"As the grandparents to six grandkids . . . two of them at a distance, Steve and I found this book both inspiring and helpful. Grandparenting at a distance can leave us feeling as if we aren't enough . . . not there enough, not doing enough, not influencing enough. The practical suggestions from Josh Mulvihill and Wayne Rice will help long-distance grandparents feel like they have a pathway to being long distance, but enough. Great read and excellent help."

—Valerie Bell, Awana CEO, and Steve Bell, executive vice president of Willow Creek Association

"Words do not adequately express the joy our grandkids have brought us and the sadness we so often feel because they live so far away. This book was a very personal read for me on several levels. Every page brought confirmation of our important role as grandparents and every page brought practical ideas that we started implementing immediately. Wayne Rice is a treasured friend and mentor in my life. I just ordered a box of these books to pass out to friends!"

—Jim Burns, PhD, president of HomeWord; author of *Doing Life with Your Adult Child: Keep Your Mouth Shut and the Welcome Mat Out*

"If you are a long-distance grandparent, this is the book for you. Use it to turn the miles between you and your grandkids from an obstacle to an opportunity. Information and activities will help you share your faith in Christ and wisdom you have gained—and have some old-fashioned FUN with your grandkids."

—David Lynn, author, trainer, and creator of HomeandChurch.com

LONG-
DISTANCE
Grandparenting

Titles in the GRANDPARENTING MATTERS Series

LONG-DISTANCE

Grandparenting

Nurturing the Faith of Your Grandchildren
When You Can't Be There in Person

WAYNE RICE

DR. JOSH MULVIHILL, GENERAL EDITOR

BETHANYHOUSE

a division of Baker Publishing Group
Minneapolis, Minnesota

© 2019 by Legacy Coalition

Published by Bethany House Publishers
11400 Hampshire Avenue South
Bloomington, Minnesota 55438
www.bethanyhouse.com

Bethany House Publishers is a division of
Baker Publishing Group, Grand Rapids, Michigan

Printed in the United States of America

Library of Congress Cataloging-in-Publication Data
Names: Rice, Wayne, author.
Title: Long-distance grandparenting : nurturing the faith of your grandchildren
    when you can't be there in person / Wayne Rice ; Josh Mulvihill, general editor.
Description: Minneapolis : Bethany House, a division of Baker Publishing Group,
    2019. | Series: Grandparenting matters
Identifiers: LCCN 2018038765| ISBN 9780764231315 (trade paper : alk. paper) |
    ISBN 9781493417421 (e-book)
Subjects: LCSH: Grandparents—Religious life. | Parenting—Religious aspects—
    Christianity. | Child rearing—Religious aspects—Christianity.
Classification: LCC BV4528.5 .R53 2019 | DDC 248.8/45—dc23
LC record available at https://lccn.loc.gov/2018038765

Cover design by Dan Pitts

Wayne Rice is represented by William Denzel.

19 20 21 22 23 24 25   7 6 5 4 3 2 1

CONTENTS

SERIES PREFACE

GRANDPARENTING MATTERS is a series of short books that address common grandparenting problems with biblical solutions and practical ideas. I have the joy of talking with grandparents all over the country about their God-designed role in the lives of children and grandchildren. Regularly, questions arise about how to do what the Bible says in the midst of barriers, problems, and challenges.

Grandparenting is filled with many joys, but it is also filled with unexpected pain and problems. Relational tensions, grandparenting restrictions, adult prodigals, grandparents as parents, divorce, long-distance relationships, and blended families all can cause the heart to ache. When brokenness touches our family, we naturally ask questions about how to navigate the challenges.

There are a growing number of resources for Christian grandparents that address the purpose of grandparenting, but few resources deal with the problem-solving side of family life. We created this series because problems are common, hope is needed, and God's Word provides guidance that can be applied to our unique situations. This series aims to simultaneously comfort and encourage, to equip and edify, as well as to point the way ahead. If you are discouraged or hurting, then I trust you will be blessed by this series. If you are looking for biblical solutions and practical how-tos, you will find them in these pages.

We've titled the series GRANDPARENTING MATTERS because we believe the Bible teaches that the grandparent-grandchild relationship is important and worthy of our time and attention. Grandparents have a significant impact on the spiritual lives of grandchildren second only to that of parents. Our prayer is that the Gospel is proclaimed, God is honored, your family experiences healing and health, and your children and children's children know, love, and serve Jesus.

I'm delighted by the high caliber of authors in this series and the impact these books will have on families for their good and for the glory of God. It has been a tremendous privilege to be partners in God's grace with these fine authors. I trust you will be blessed by their godly wisdom, gain a renewed hope in God, experience joy in Christ despite trying circumstances, and be better equipped to be a disciple-making grandparent who passes on a heritage of faith to future generations.

Josh Mulvihill
Founding Member, the Legacy Coalition
Executive Director of Church
and Family Ministry, Renewanation
Connect with me at GospelShapedFamily.com.

INTRODUCTION

I think we can all agree that one of the great joys of growing older is becoming a grandparent!

And sadly, one of the great heartbreaks of grandparenting is when you are separated from your grandchildren for lengthy periods.

They live in another town or another state or even another country. Maybe their mom and dad had to move because of a job opportunity or a military deployment. Or it could have been other family issues (perhaps they moved to be closer to the in-laws), or they had to find more affordable housing, or better weather, or better schools, or better doctors.

Or maybe it was you who had to relocate and suddenly you found yourself many miles away from your children and grandchildren. That can happen too—sometimes by choice, and other times out of necessity.

Obviously there are plenty of good (and not so good) reasons why we become long-distance grandparents. In today's mobile society, it's very easy these days, and rather likely, for families to move several times during their working years and to move great distances as well. I'll tell you a little bit about my own family's story shortly.

In recent years I have been working closely with the Legacy Coalition—a ministry to and for grandparents—and I have come to appreciate greatly that the biblical role of a grandparent is much more than just being a playmate or baby-sitter. I love to take our grandkids fishing or go on hikes or play games with them, but I now have come to realize that grandparents also have a holy calling and responsibility to pass on a legacy of faith to their grandchildren. More on this later, but suffice it to say that this realization has been a game changer for me.

So, I've found that becoming a long-distance grandparent can make you not only sad but it can be rather challenging as well. How can you be a spiritual influence on your grandchildren when you rarely ever see them? That's the reason for this book.

The Distance Dilemma

Here's what I've learned so far about long-distance grandparenting.

Simply put, you can choose one of three ways to respond to distance.

1. Distance can become an *excuse* for not doing anything. It's easy to just throw up our hands and say that because we live far away from our grandchildren, there's nothing we can do. We are now exempt from our responsibility to influence our grandchildren for Christ. We're off the hook, so to speak. Sadly, many grandparents take this approach.
2. Distance can be seen as an *obstacle*. We have good intentions but let the distance prevent us from doing anything.

It's just too big an obstacle to overcome. We let it stand in the way of being the kind of spiritual influence on our grandchildren that God wants us to be.

3. Or, distance can be an *opportunity*. I have learned that it is possible for grandparents who live far away from their grandchildren to actually have a better relationship with their grandchildren than those who live close by. Some grandparents take proximity to their grandchildren for granted! Long-distance grandparents, on the other hand, *have* to be intentional about connecting with grandchildren, and doing so with regularity.

Distance does not have to be an excuse or an obstacle to good grandparenting. I know from experience that long-distance grandparents can make a deep and lasting impression that goes on for generations. And they provide a special kind of love that no one else can duplicate. It would be nice if all grandparents could live within walking distance of all their grandchildren and have easy access to them, but in today's world, that is rarely the case. Therefore, we should try to be the most intentional, loving, and effective grandparents that we can possibly be.

Ideas, Ideas!

I've tried to make this book as practical as possible, so it contains a lot of ideas that I have collected from other grandparents. Here are three bits of advice concerning them:

1. Don't try them all. If you do, your grandkids will think you've gone crazy.
2. Don't let any of these ideas make you feel guilty about everything you are not doing. Remember that in most cases, *something is always better than nothing.* None of

us were perfect parents and we're not going to be perfect grandparents either. But we can all probably do a little better than we're doing right now. So choose something you can do rather than feel bad about all you're not doing.

3. If an idea sounds good but doesn't quite fit your situation, change it. No idea is very good right out of the box. As you read through these ideas, think how you might be able to adapt them to fit your family, your personality, or your grandkids. Hopefully, these suggestions can help you think of other great ideas that aren't in this book.

Thanks

Thanks, Josh Mulvihill, for asking me to write this book as part of a series of grandparenting books for Bethany House and the Legacy Coalition. The whole process of gathering ideas and thinking deeply about this subject has been very motivating for me. I have realized how much I love my grandchildren, and there's nothing more I would like for them to know than that God loves them too—even more than Grandpa does.

Thank you to Deborah Haddix, an experienced grandma and author who generously sent me a batch of great ideas, many of which are included throughout this book. Thanks also to my cousin Justin Rice, who has been a great encouragement to me and a wonderful example of what good grandparenting looks like.

Thanks to Larry Fowler and the entire Legacy Coalition team for giving me the opportunity to serve in this very important ministry to grandparents. As my old friend John Coulombe likes to say, "If things are going to get better in this country, it's not about changing what happens in the White House; it's about changing what happens in *our* house." Amen, brother.

1

On Becoming a Long-Distance Grandparent

My grandparents were long-distance grandparents.

As a child, I probably thought that *all* grandparents lived far away simply because that was my experience. In reality, long-distance grandparenting is a relatively recent development. While researchers tell us that more than half of all grandparents today have grandchildren who live more than 200 miles away from them, this has not always been the case.[1] Before World War II, the typical American household[2] included one or more grandparents living under the same roof as their children and grandchildren. It was more typical for grandparents of a few generations ago to be close to their grandkids than to be far away.

But that was not the case for me.

I was born on the front edge of the baby boom. Immediately after World War II, my newly-discharged-from-the-navy father made the decision to move his young family from Tennessee, where I was born, to California, where I have lived ever since. His decision to move west was primarily an economic one, and it paid off handsomely as my father became a successful building contractor in fledgling Ventura County, just north of the city of Los Angeles.

Because we lived so far out west, I rarely ever saw my grandparents. We did, however, make the pilgrimage each summer from California to Tennessee to visit the "kinfolk"—including my grandparents. I have (mostly) fond memories of those three- and four-day drives in the desert heat across the U.S. on two-lane highway Route 66, sandwiched in the backseat of our Oldsmobile between my two brothers, without air conditioning or entertainment of any kind save the occasional string of Burma Shave signs that would appear along the highway or a stop at a genuine Indian Trading Post. As a child, the word *vacation* was pretty much synonymous with visiting relatives—much more so than going to amusement parks or camping trips.

I'm thankful that my parents made those treks across the country a priority during my childhood years. For that reason, my grandparents were not completely unknown to me, and while they didn't have the opportunity to spend a lot of time with me, I learned much from them during those visits, especially about my heritage as a Christian.

For example, I have vivid memories of our visits to the home of my great-grandparents, "Pappy" and "Mammy" Nesbitt. These were my mother's grandparents who lived in the "country." I put the word *country* in quotation marks because "country" people in Tennessee were true hillbillies who were different from people who lived in the city. They had no modern conveniences except for maybe a telephone and a radio. They lived off the land, gathered eggs from the henhouse, milked the cows, plowed the fields (with mules rather than tractors), and generally worked hard their entire lives. Life expectancy was not long, so I was quite fortunate that my Pappy and Mammy Nesbitt were still alive.

Of course, a visit to the country was a real adventure for a California boy like me. First, in order to get to Pappy Nesbitt's house (which was actually a cabin), we had to drive down several miles of dirt roads until we reached the "holler" where they lived. Then we hiked down a path that led to the creek and the swinging bridge that crossed it and led to their home. The bridge was made of poles on each side of the creek, thick ropes, and wooden slats, handmade, no doubt, by Pappy himself. It would sway back and forth as we crossed over to the other side. I loved playing on that bridge.

This was also my first experience using a "privy" (or outhouse). Of course, country people did not have indoor plumbing. They had a water well behind the cabin from which they drew water up in buckets for cooking, baths, washing clothes, etc. All this was fascinating to me. The world I lived in was nothing like this one.

Perhaps my most indelible memory of my great-grandparents, however, was listening to them sing and pray. Whenever we would visit, they always took time to sing and pray with us. It was not like the singing and praying I was used to. They came from a holiness church background, which apparently assumed that God was hard of hearing because they prayed and sang as loud as they could. They would also "get happy" with shouts of joy and often tears. As a child it was a little bit scary for me, but it also made a big impression.

So much so that my brother Jim wrote a country song based on our experiences visiting our Nesbitt grandparents. If you'd like to hear the music, search iTunes or YouTube for "Swingin' Bridge" by the group Brush Arbor.

> 1. I was just a young boy, playing on that swingin' bridge
> Out at Granpappy Nesbitt's house through the creek and
>   over the ridge
> Laughin' out loud on that old bridge, us kids could make
>   it swing
> And we could hear comin' from the house the old folks as
>   they'd sing

CHORUS:
Swingin' bridge
Memories of how we used to pray
Somehow deep inside my soul, all I am and all I know
Traces back to the days of that swingin' bridge.

2. Throwin' rocks to the water below I could hear Amazing Grace
And I can picture Granpappy sing as the tears rolled down
his face
He'd call us kids together knowing that we'd rather play
But there's no way he'd let us leave without some time to
pray . . .

3. All us kids are married now with children of our own
And each of us made the good Lord the foundation of our
home
And in my mind I often drive through the creek and over
the ridge
To play and sing Amazing Grace, on that old swingin'
bridge.[3]

Here's the point: Long-distance grandparents can still have
a powerful impact on their grandchildren even when they don't
see them all that often. I only saw my grandparents once a
year (at best), but I will never forget them and I will always be
grateful for their love and faithfulness to Christ, which is now
being replicated in the lives of their grandchildren and great-
grandchildren and beyond. This will always be a comfort to me
because I am now a long-distance grandparent myself.

When the Grandchildren Move Away

My wife, Marci, and I couldn't hold back the tears when the
last of our three children and their families moved away from

San Diego and our "home place" where they grew up and where we still live. Our son Nathan and his family (including our two oldest grandchildren) have never lived close to us, but for many years they were only a two-hour drive away. Now they live in Seattle, Washington, more than 1,200 miles away, where Nate is a youth pastor and family counselor. Our daughter, Amber, just this year joined her brother in Seattle, where she found employment as a marriage and family therapist, and she took her son Jack (our next-oldest grandchild) with her of course. Our son Corey, along with his wife and our two youngest grandchildren, also moved away just a few months before Amber did, although not quite so far away. They currently live in Hollister, California, which is about 450 miles from San Diego. We can make that drive in about seven hours and have done so several times already. All three of our children moved to these distant locations for reasons of employment, which was necessary and completely understandable even though it hurt deeply to see them go. This has resulted in a big change for us. Our home was for so many years a hubbub of activity for our whole family. For a while, our daughter and grandson Jack lived with us during a transition time in her life (she is a single mom).

Now my wife and I are alone, and while we know it wasn't intentional on the part of our kids, we sometimes feel a bit abandoned. I use that term jokingly of course—our kids didn't deliberately try to get away from us (at least we hope not). Still, we miss them all greatly and sometimes feel envious of grandparents we know who have easy access to their grandchildren all year long.

Responding Appropriately

As I mentioned, Marci and I had quite a few mixed emotions when the last of our children (and grandchildren) moved away from us. We were very sad because we were losing them, but at the same time we were happy that they were able to live their own lives and had some good opportunities awaiting them elsewhere. We also experienced dread, disappointment, anxiety—even a little anger at times. Why did they have to leave us now? Couldn't they have waited a few more years? Was this really necessary?

Feelings of loss and sadness are to be expected, that's true. But one thing we've learned is that we don't want to let our feelings ruin the relationships we have with our kids and grandkids. We don't want how we feel to become a heavy burden for them to bear. Some grandparents go out of their way to remind their children constantly that they are sad and lonely. Maybe that's why the kids moved away in the first place—they just got tired of being around someone who complains or criticizes them all the time. If you keep a scorecard on how many times they visit or call, you can be sure that you will get fewer visits and calls. Scorekeeping only puts pressure on the relationship, which is completely counterproductive.

If you want your children and grandchildren to reach out to you more often, be the most positive, encouraging, grace-filled parent and grandparent you can be. It's okay to be honest with your kids and grandkids from time to time, but don't make your own misery the main topic of conversation every time they call or they will definitely stop calling. Instead, learn to forgive, focus on the positive, and enjoy your family every time you have the opportunity. Ask questions and focus on their feelings more than your own and you will definitely get a lot more calls and visits.

When Grandparents Do the Leaving

Besides employment or deployment, our children and grandchildren can move away for any number of personal or professional reasons. But sometimes it's not the children who do the leaving—it's us! Nowadays it's becoming more and more common for retirees to pick up and move off to a distant place where the weather is better, the cost of living is lower, and the golf courses are plentiful. The "retirement lifestyle" has now become a big part of the American Dream—that golden age when you can finally stop working and begin ticking items off your bucket list. Or, you can move to a nice adults-only community where you can pursue the life of leisure you've always wanted.

It all sounds wonderful—and for many people it is—but now it's the children and grandchildren who are likely to feel abandoned. Just when the grandkids need the wisdom and influence that only a grandparent can bring, Grandpa and Grandma have flown the coop. They've either sequestered themselves in Florida where they are living the good life, or they are sunning themselves on the deck of a cruise ship in the Caribbean.

Due to the aging of the baby boomer generation, the fifty-five and older gated community has become the fastest-growing housing trend in America today. Some of these communities, such as The Villages[4] in Florida, don't allow anyone under nineteen to live there and restrict visits by children to a maximum of thirty days a year. Not all of these communities are quite so restrictive, but they all pitch "the good life" as one of leisure rather than one of legacy and responsibility.

The only hope we have that our children and grandchildren will have faith is for us to pass it on to them without regard for our own comfort and convenience. How can we impart our knowledge and our experience with God to them when we have isolated ourselves in a gated community in a galaxy far away?

I know that circumstances as well as proper stewardship of time and resources often require us to make changes in where and how we live after retirement. My wife and I recently downsized to a smaller home in our area after more than forty years in the same house. We had to sell the old home place, which was a difficult thing to do because that was where we had raised our children and hosted so many gatherings of friends and family over the years. We said goodbye to a place with so many good memories, but we now have something we can afford on our much smaller income. But it's not a community for seniors only. Our next-door neighbors have children, and we do have a spare bedroom where the grandchildren can stay for as long as they want.

The Bucket-List Retirement

And then there's the bucket list. It was popularized in the 2007 movie about two terminally ill men (played by Jack Nicholson and Morgan Freeman) who meet in the hospital and set out on a quest to complete their combined bucket list, which includes visiting Stonehenge and getting a tattoo. The movie was intended to be a comedy—and it does have its very funny moments—but the concept has been taken quite seriously by a lot of retirees (and grandparents), who are unabashedly "spending their children's inheritance" by doing all the things they were unable to do when they were younger.

Psychiatrist Marc Agronin, in an article he wrote for the *Wall Street Journal*, states, "For many seniors, the bucket list has become the ultimate celebration of aging." He describes how today's generation of retirees (who have more money than ever before) are spending their golden years chasing once-in-a-lifetime adventures like sky diving from 13,000 feet, hiking the Great Wall of China, swimming with sharks, or skiing the Andes. For them, it's the chance to do things they put off for years while working and caring for family, and to make the most of the time they have remaining. "What's not to love about a life of dream vacations and big thrills?" he asks.

"Unfortunately, quite a lot," responds Dr. Agronin, answering his own question. He explains how he, as a therapist, has

22

had conversations with numerous seniors who say that rather than feeling exhilarated by a life of bucket-list adventures, they often end up feeling depressed and disconnected. He recommends that seniors stay home and do something meaningful and productive with their lives instead, or take their grandchildren with them on their bucket-list adventures so they can spend some quality time with them or teach them something new.[5]

Gated retirement communities and bucket list adventures are marketed heavily these days to aging baby boomers who haven't given much thought to their roles and responsibilities as grandparents and the consequences of taking extended time away from their grandkids. As I mentioned earlier, there are many good reasons why we become long-distance grandparents and some of them are completely out of our control. But when we do have the choice and opportunity to avoid putting distance between ourselves and our grandchildren, we are wise to do all we can to stay close by and connected.

Distance Isn't Always Measured in Miles

You don't have to be hundreds of miles away from your grandchildren to be a long-distance grandparent, of course. If you live in Los Angeles for example, it might take an hour to go visit your grandchildren even though they live in the same city. And even if you don't have traffic issues, it's possible for people to live very near, even on the same street, and never have any contact with each other. I have a friend who lives very close to me whom I never see except once a year at a conference we both attend some 2,000 miles away. We always laugh when we see each other because it seems crazy that we don't connect more often at home. Just because you live close to someone doesn't mean that you will be spending a lot of time with them. I'm embarrassed to admit that even when our grandchildren lived close to us, we sometimes went weeks without seeing them. We had to make a real effort to go visit or to invite them to our home.

There are lots of reasons for why and how we become long-distance grandparents—some good, some not so good—but if we understand the role of a grandparent from a biblical perspective, distance doesn't have to be a barrier to good grandparenting. It is to the biblical role of a grandparent that we now turn.

For Further Reflection and Action

1. Did you have long-distance grandparents? How did they influence you?
2. How does being a long-distance grandparent make you feel?
3. How do you plan to spend your retirement years?
4. Do you have a bucket list? What's on it?
5. Try creating a bucket list of things you want to do with each of your grandchildren during the next five years. Start checking those items off your list as soon as you can!

The Biblical Role of a Grandparent

- "If I had known how much fun grandkids could be, I'd have had them first."
- "I love being a grandparent. You get to spoil them and then send them back home."
- "Grandmas never run out of hugs or cookies."
- "The simplest toy, one which even the youngest child can operate, is called a grandparent."

The popular role of a grandparent has in recent years transitioned from being a wise and respected family patriarch or matriarch to that of being a grand baby-sitter and playmate for the grandkids. Today's grandparents are not expected to be involved very much in the teaching, training, or spiritual lives of grandchildren because they are more than likely "making the most of their retirement years," and besides, it's best for grandparents not to interfere too much in the family lives of their children. So at best, today's grandparents must be content with providing hugs, cookies, child care, and an appreciative audience to play to now and then. We show up at birthday parties and soccer games and do our best to cheer them on—and make fools of ourselves if necessary.

When a grandparent's role seems so unimportant, it's not surprising that some grandparents don't even bother to do those things in their prescribed role with any degree of consistency or passion.

But maybe there's more to being a grandparent—a lot more—something far more rewarding and significant.

As it turns out, the Bible has quite a lot to say about what grandparents are supposed to be and do. Just as the Bible is pretty specific about the roles and responsibilities of other family members (such as husbands, wives, and children), so the Bible has some very specific things to say about grandparenting. And we find quite a few examples of grandparenting in the Bible as well.

My friend and colleague Josh Mulvihill wrote his PhD dissertation on this very subject. In his book *Biblical Grandparenting*, he unpacks the many Scriptures that apply to grandparents and concludes that the key word describing a grandparent's role is the word *heritage*.[1] Grandparents who have faith in God are to pass that faith on to their children—as well as their grandchildren—as an inheritance or *heritage*. This is how faith gets passed down through the generations. It has been said that the Christian faith is always one generation away from extinction. That may sound like an overstatement, but there is never a guarantee that the faith we have received from our parents, grandparents, or past generations of Christians will survive us—unless we pass it on.

Perhaps the most compelling verse in the Bible regarding a grandparent's role is found in Deuteronomy 4:9 where we are instructed to teach the things of God "to your children and to their children after them."

Some versions of the Bible translate it "to your children and also your grandchildren" or "to your children and your children's children." However it's translated, it's very clear that God is commanding His people here to not only pass faith on to their children but the generation that is coming up behind their children as well. As a parent, you aren't finished when you've done your best to teach your children to love and serve God. If your children have children, you get the responsibility—and the privilege—of teaching these things to them also.

This actually makes a lot of sense, doesn't it? A great deal of research has been done in the last thirty years to determine who or what has the greatest influence on the values and religious beliefs of young people. Over and over, researchers have confirmed that *parents* rank number one among the many influences competing for the attention and allegiance of our children and youth. Parents are more influential than teachers, peers, the internet, TV, rock music, celebrities, you name it. When I was working with students in youth ministry, I was always hoping one of these researchers would also find that youth pastors had a growing influence on the values and beliefs of young people, but I was always disappointed. Parents always came in first. Youth pastors and other adults are found further down the list.

But who or what came in second place? The research always found that right behind parents were *grandparents*—the extended family. It's clear that God in His wisdom has given the responsibility for teaching children the truth of His Word not to professional teachers or media stars, but to parents and grandparents. They hold the keys to the kingdom in the eyes of their children and grandchildren. The family is the most important classroom in a child's life—where they learn best what's important in their life. If parents and grandparents are faithful about passing faith on, there is a high degree of probability that their children and grandchildren will follow in the way they have been taught for the rest of their lives (Proverbs 22:6).

If this can be compared to a relay race, with each generation passing the baton of faith on to the next, we can find instances in the Bible when one generation dropped the baton completely, leaving subsequent generations with no faith at all. The first few chapters of the book of Judges are a good example of this:

> After that whole generation had been gathered to their ancestors, another generation grew up who knew neither the Lord nor what he had done for Israel. Then the Israelites did evil in the eyes of the Lord and served the Baals. They forsook the Lord, the God of their ancestors, who had brought them out of Egypt. They followed and worshiped various gods of the peoples around them.
>
> Judges 2:10–12

This had serious consequences for Israel, as they no longer had the protection and blessing of God upon them, and they suffered greatly. We don't know exactly what went wrong here, but it's clear that a generation of Israelites grew up "who neither knew the Lord nor what he had done for Israel." Somehow, the stories of God's faithfulness and goodness were never told; the lessons were never taught. This was a colossal failure on the part of their parents and grandparents.

Again, we see a little later in the history of Israel:

> They would not listen, however, but persisted in their former practices. Even while these people were worshiping the Lord, they were serving their idols. To this day their children and grandchildren continue to do as their ancestors did.
>
> 2 Kings 17:40–41

In today's very individualistic culture, we tend to minimize the impact or influence of our ancestors, but the Bible makes quite clear that there is a strong connection between the decisions we make today and outcomes that can impact many generations that follow us.

I, for one, am very grateful for the heritage of faith that has been passed along to me because of decisions made by my parents, grandparents, and even great-great-grandparents. Several years ago I attended a family reunion at which one of our cousins had painstakingly drawn on the wall a carefully researched family tree that went back several generations. Stories were told about our grandparents and great-grandparents—and I was astounded to find that quite a few of my ancestors had been called to preach or to plant a church or to teach at a Christian college. As I was learning about my family, the thought kept running through my head, *No wonder I do what I do*. It almost seems inevitable that I would also be called to ministry, given the number of people in my family's history who were. My parents never pushed any of this on me. On the contrary, they encouraged me to choose my own path. But the pull of serving Christ in full-time ministry was always there below the surface it seems, perhaps because of the long-ago prayers and patterns of godly ancestors.

Some Key Bible Verses

If you do a search for the word *grandparent* (or *grandfather* or *grandmother*) in the Bible, you won't find too many verses using those exact words. Josh Mulvihill points out that these words only occur twice in all of Scripture—one verse each in the Old and New Testaments: (1) "And they [locusts] shall fill your houses and the houses of all your servants and of all the Egyptians, as neither your fathers nor your *grandfathers* have seen, from the day they came on the earth to this day" (Exodus 10:6 ESV, emphasis added). (2) "I am reminded of your sincere faith, a faith that dwelt first in your *grandmother* Lois and your mother Eunice and now, I am sure, dwells in you as well." (2 Timothy 1:5 ESV, emphasis added).[2]

But just because the Bible doesn't mention grandparents specifically doesn't mean the Bible doesn't have grandparents in mind throughout Scripture. Often the Bible references grandparents with terms like *father of his father*, *forefathers*, *father's father*, *God of your fathers*, and so on. Grandchildren are often referenced with terms like *children's children* or *generation after generation*, etc. Similarly, when the Bible discusses old age, there are many applications to grandparenthood. For example, Proverbs 17:6 states, "Grandchildren are the crowning glory of the aged" (NLT). Even though we may not consider ourselves "aged," most grandparents do qualify as having "old age" or being an "elder."

As I mentioned earlier, probably the most direct grandparenting passage in the Bible is found in Deuteronomy 4:9. Here it is in its entirety:

> Only be careful, and watch yourselves closely so that you do not forget the things your eyes have seen or let them fade from your heart as long as you live. Teach them to your children and to their children after them.

The key word in that passage is *and*. For many years, I taught parents that they should teach their children about God but never noticed that word *and* in reference to the next generation. Clearly, our job as teachers is not finished when our children grow up and leave home. The biblical pattern is for parents to teach both their children *and* their grandchildren. This is not limited to grandparents whose children are nearby; it also applies to long-distance grandparents. There are many ways for us to teach and have an influence across the miles, as we shall see.

Another passage that I have appreciated for years and have quoted many times is found in Psalm 71. Verses 17 and 18 read this way:

> Since my youth, God, you have taught me,
>> and to this day I declare your marvelous deeds.
> Even when I am old and gray,
>> do not forsake me, my God,
> till I declare your power to the next generation,
>> your mighty acts to all who are to come.

These verses kept me in youth ministry for many years—even long after I was "old and gray." As a grandparent now, I see how it also applies to those of us who have grown children and grandchildren. In most cases when the Bible speaks of the "next generation," it is referring to our immediate families. "All who are to come" is a reference to our children's children, namely our grandchildren and great-grandchildren. Taking responsibility for passing faith on to our family first has always been taught, even if not assumed, in Scripture. I like to call this our "First Commission" (in contrast to the Great Commission of Matthew 28). Before Jesus gave His disciples the Great Commission (to take the Gospel to the whole world), God gave us the First Commission—to pass faith on to our children and grandchildren.

Another important grandparenting passage is found in Psalm 78:5–7:

> He decreed statutes for Jacob
>> and established the law in Israel
> which he commanded our ancestors
>> to teach their children,
> so the next generation would know them,
>> even the children yet to be born,
>> and they in turn would tell their children.
> Then they would put their trust in God
>> and would not forget his deeds
>> but would keep his commands.

31

In these verses, we see that the primary job description for grandparents (ancestors) is summed up with the word "teach." There are many ways to accomplish this of course (we'll look at some ways in the following chapters), but there's no question that God expects parents and grandparents to be the primary Christian educators of their children and grandchildren—so that they will learn to put their trust in God and follow Jesus. There's no room here for outsourcing this to others or just hoping and praying that it will somehow happen on its own. Grandparents are given a very specific job to do.

Another passage that definitely speaks to grandparents is this one from Psalm 92:12–15:

> The righteous will flourish like a palm tree,
>   they will grow like a cedar of Lebanon;
> planted in the house of the Lord,
>   they will flourish in the courts of our God.
> They will still bear fruit in old age;
>   they will stay fresh and green,
> proclaiming, "The Lord is upright;
>   he is my Rock and there is no wickedness in him."

While there is no direct reference to grandparenting here, this is a very encouraging passage for all of us. No matter how old we are, we can continue to grow in our faith and bear fruit. Our grandparenting years were never meant to be a time for cruising downhill or calling it quits. Instead, these years can be a time for renewed spiritual growth and a reorienting of priorities. Perhaps we didn't do such a great parenting job when we were younger. Well, as my friend Tim Kimmel puts it, now it's time to "play a mulligan."[3] In other words, you get a do-over. And that can be taken in many different ways. Maybe you were just too busy with job and family and demands on your time to focus much on your own spiritual journey. Perhaps now is the time to begin practicing the kind of spiritual disciplines that can help you know and love Christ in a deeper and more personal way. You can "flourish in the courts of God" by spending time with Jesus and learning to do the things that He taught His disciples to do. This is one area where the phrase "You're not getting older, you're getting better" actually applies. We can continue to become more and more like Jesus for the rest of our lives. And when you are doing this, you can't help but bear fruit in the lives of your family members, which of course includes your grandchildren—no matter whether they are close or far away.

Biblical Guidelines for Grandparents

In Paul's letter to Titus, the apostle offers a number of behavioral standards for the more mature members of God's family, the church. These standards can certainly be applied to us today:

> Older men are to be temperate, dignified, sensible, sound in faith, in love, in perseverance. Older women likewise are to be reverent in their behavior, not malicious gossips nor enslaved to much wine, teaching what is good, so that they may encourage the young women.
>
> Titus 2:2–4 NASB

From this instruction, we learn that grandfathers should be:

- "Temperate"—that is, sober in judgment, self-controlled.
- "Dignified"—also translated as "serious" or "respected." That doesn't mean being boring, stodgy, or aloof, but rather being worthy of admiration.
- "Sound in faith"—having a genuine relationship with Christ that is unshakeable.

- "Sound in love"—being someone who is generous with God's love. One of the dangers of growing old is that we become critical, cynical, fault-finding. A godly grandparent models and expresses God's love for everyone.
- "Sound in perseverance"—sometimes translated "patience," which sometimes is not easy when you get older. Age, however, provides perspective, and for the believer, we have hope in Christ that gives us patience and perseverance through difficult times.

Likewise, Paul suggests that grandmothers be:

- "Reverent in behavior"—genuine in their faith and putting into practice what they believe. They should live their lives in such a way that others know they are serious about their faith in Christ.
- "Not a malicious gossip"—careful not to say bad things about other people.
- "Not enslaved to much wine"—which may have been a serious problem with the women of Crete when Paul wrote his letter to Titus, and it is no less a problem today of course. A godly grandmother will be careful to avoid addiction to harmful substances like alcohol or drugs.
- "Teaching what is good"—taking every opportunity to instruct younger women—especially children and grandchildren—about the joys and responsibilities of following Christ.

There are many other places to go in the Bible to learn what God expects of grandparents (as well as all of Christ's disciples as they mature and get older). For example, Galatians 5:22–23 (ESV) tells us about the kind of fruit we should be producing as a result of God's Spirit working in us over the years: "love, joy, peace, patience, kindness, goodness, faithfulness, gentleness, self-control." These are all qualities that we should desire and cultivate in our lives so we can model Christlikeness in front of our grandchildren whenever we have the opportunity.

Does the Bible have anything specific to say about long-distance grandparenting? The answer to that question would be no. The kind of mobility that is possible for family members today did not exist in biblical times. But we can learn from the example of Paul himself, who was often separated from his church family as he traveled around the known world and when he was being held in a prison cell. He didn't let circumstances discourage him from reaching out to his "children" (1 Thessalonians 2:7) however he could—with visits, letters, and couriers—to contact, encourage, and strengthen his spiritual children in the faith. Likewise, long-distance grandparents can use every means at our disposal to visit and communicate regularly with our grandchildren so we can leverage the love and godly concern that we have for them. Being separated from our grandchildren does not give us a pass from fulfilling our God-given responsibilities as grandparents.

Letting Go and Letting God

While there can be no doubt that the Bible encourages—dare I say even *commands*—us to continue to be involved in the spiritual formation of our grandchildren, it is not God's intention to burden us with another source of worry or guilt. There is only so much we can do. Long-distance grandparents are especially vulnerable to feelings of anxiety and discouragement caused by separation from their children and grandchildren. This is not what God wants for you or for me.

Instead, God wants us to trust Him, to rely upon Him for everything, especially for our families. We are not in control.

We are not the ones who will determine what our children and grandchildren believe or how they choose to live their lives.

But we can trust God. Christian philosopher and author Dallas Willard once said about parenting, "You know you never get over being a parent. You can't divorce your kids. But you can surrender them to God. You can give them to God. And it is one of the greatest challenges of parents to do that. You have to surrender your children to God."[4]

This is of course part of our own spiritual journey as we come to love Jesus more and learn how to surrender ourselves completely to His will. This is one of our deepest acts of love: to trust God completely with not only our own lives but with the lives of our kids and grandkids as well.

For Further Reflection and Action

1. What is the heritage you would most like to pass on to your grandchildren?
2. Psalm 92 says that we can "bear fruit" in old age. What is the fruit you would like to bear during the fourth quarter of your life?
3. Of the biblical guidelines for older people described in the book of Titus, which describes you best? Which of them is a growth area for you?
4. Do a Bible study of your own (or with a small group) on biblical grandparenting. Find out what the Bible has to say not only about grandparenting but also about how you can thrive and bear fruit in the last quarter of your life.

3

The Prayer Connection

The prayer of a righteous person is powerful and effective. Elijah was a human being, even as we are. He prayed earnestly that it would not rain, and it did not rain on the land for three and a half years. Again he prayed, and the heavens gave rain, and the earth produced its crops.

James 5:16–18

The most important and reliable connection between a long-distance grandparent and his or her grandchildren is prayer. Even though you are far away from them, prayer can bring you and your grandkids together in a significant and powerful way. With God, there is no distance at all between us and our grandkids.

In the Scripture passage above, notice that Elijah prayed very specific prayers: "Lord, stop the rain!" and "Lord, let it pour!" And his prayers were answered. James points out that Elijah was a human being just like us! God listened to him and answered his prayers. Likewise, we can pray specifically for our grandchildren—by name and by need—and our prayers will be effective. Even though we are many miles away from our grandchildren, we can close the distance with our prayers for them.

Many of the books I have collected over the years on parenting (and grandparenting) add a chapter on prayer at the end—as if prayer is a last resort or an afterthought. I am putting this chapter on prayer early in this book because it is not a last resort at all. Prayer is the most important thing that a grandparent can do for his or her grandchildren. As grandparents, we do not have much say in our grandchildren's lives, but we can pray that God will, in His grace and mercy, be present with them and guide them along their way. We can pray for specific needs they have and particular concerns we have. And God will be faithful because the prayers of a righteous grandparent can accomplish much. I believe that most grandchildren desire the prayers of their grandparents even more than they want their cookies or Christmas gifts. When grandchildren know that their grandparents are praying for them, they feel secure and loved in a way that goes far beyond the value of money or things.

So how can we pray effectively for our grandchildren?

My friend Paul Sailhamer shared with me a very helpful template on intercessory prayer that is based on a model prayer from the Bible.[1] In Colossians 1:9–14, we are allowed to listen in on one of Paul's prayers for his spiritual children in Colossae. In this prayer are a number of cues for us to pray for our children and especially for our grandchildren.

> For this reason, since the day we heard about you, we have not stopped praying for you. We continually ask God to fill you with the knowledge of his will through all the wisdom and understanding that the Spirit gives, so that you may live a life worthy of the Lord and please him in every way: bearing fruit in every good work, growing in the knowledge of God, being

strengthened with all power according to his glorious might so that you may have great endurance and patience, and giving joyful thanks to the Father, who has qualified you to share in the inheritance of his holy people in the kingdom of light. For he has rescued us from the dominion of darkness and brought us into the kingdom of the Son he loves, in whom we have redemption, the forgiveness of sins.

Colossians 1:9–14

The first thing we learn here about intercessory prayer is that it is extremely urgent. Paul says that from the first day he heard about these fellow believers in Colossae, he began praying for them and hasn't stopped! Paul didn't rely on his charisma, his preaching ability, his personality, or even his ability to perform miracles. His first move was to begin praying for these people—continuously. We learn here that effective prayer for our grandchildren must be consistent and earnest. It's a lifetime responsibility. Even when they are away from our immediate presence, as the Colossian Christians were from Paul, prayer influences their attitudes, behavior, and well-being. Prayer is a powerful tool that grandparents can't afford to be without!

What Paul asked on behalf of the Colossians provides a basic framework for our prayers on behalf of our grandchildren. This framework can keep our prayers from becoming merely repetitious and crisis-centered. Rather than simply praying, "Lord, bless our grandkids and keep them out of harm's way," we can pray for the things that we know God wants for them. They are outlined for us in this prayer by the apostle Paul.

First, we can pray that our grandchildren grow up filled with the knowledge of God's will in all spiritual wisdom and understanding. Isn't that what we want for our grandchildren? Doesn't that pretty much sum things up?

What more could we want for our grandchildren than that they grow up with *God's will* as the controlling influence of their lives? There are so many competing world views vying for the hearts and minds of our grandchildren today. Our first prayer should be that they will have the spiritual wisdom to know how to think Christianly and to discern good from bad, true from false, right from wrong, beautiful from ugly.

The world has one way of understanding these things, and God has another. That's why we pray that our grandchildren will also have godly understanding, which will not only give them the right way of thinking but the right way of responding. That's what Paul prayed for his spiritual children—he wanted them to have a godly grasp on life that would be applied practically and daily to life's choices.

Paul details the distinctives of that kind of life in the rest of his prayer (vv. 10–14). This can provide a pattern for us to pray more specifically for our grandchildren:

- **Their lifestyle**—that they might "live a life worthy of the Lord and please him in every way." All of us make lifestyle choices, and your grandkids will do the same. As you pray for your grandchildren, make a list of the specific areas of their lives that you pray will be pleasing to the Lord. Allow this list to grow and change as your grandkids grow and change.

- **The productivity of their lives**—that they are "bearing fruit in every good work." It's never too early to start praying that our grandchildren will find good and valuable ways to invest their lives, ways that will bear not only temporal but everlasting fruit. We can not only pray for their future productivity but we can encourage them along the way by pointing out and affirming their strengths, their talents, and their capabilities, and we can offer advice and mentoring when appropriate.

- **Their walk with God**—that they are "growing in the knowledge of God." We can pray that our grandchildren will continue to know Jesus in more than a superficial way. True knowledge has to do with personal experience and the intimacy of a relationship. There are many young people who grow up in the church and know a lot about God, but they don't really know God. Pray that your grandchildren will come to know Christ in a very personal way and walk with Him every day of their lives. I am personally convinced that I continued through my young adult years to seek God's best for my life because of the constant, fervent prayers of family members and committed friends who didn't let a day go by without my life being brought before the Lord.

- **That they might know how to apply God's strength to their struggles**—"being strengthened with all power according to his glorious might." God is able to provide His power and might during tough times. As grandparents, we can pray very specifically for the struggles and decisions our grandchildren are facing. If you are aware of what they are, write them down and pray that your grandchildren will rely upon God to apply His mighty power to every situation.

- **That they might be able to withstand difficult circumstances and difficult people**—so they "may have great endurance and patience." In this verse, Paul uses two words for patience. Endurance (or steadfastness) is the stamina to hang in there when things get tough. Patience is the long fuse that doesn't explode in reaction to difficult people. Pray that your grandchildren will be able to stay calm and bear with one another even when others are being unkind or unreasonable.

- **Their attitude**—that they are "giving joyful thanks to the Father." Paul desired his spiritual children to have an attitude of joyful thanksgiving. As a grandparent, I can't think of anything that would sum up my hope for my grandchildren more than that they would lead lives that express true joyfulness and genuine thanksgiving.

- **Their self-image**—that they understand God has qualified them "to share in the inheritance of his holy people in the kingdom of light." Self-image is a huge issue for today's young people. Children are always jockeying for position, sizing themselves up against their peers and pop culture heroes, their parents, mentors, and the media. Our grand-kids can make it in life if they have the proper perspective of who they really are: that God is their heavenly Father and that He has qualified them to share in His inheritance forever.

This Pauline prayer provides a framework for effective prayers of both parents and grandparents. All of the particulars of our prayers for our grandchildren and their unique circumstances and personalities can be built on this superstructure. Paul's desire for his Colossian children was that they might eventually become "complete in Christ" (1:28–29 NASB). Toward that goal he labored, and much of that labor was prayer. Should we do any less for our grandchildren?

Staying Connected by Prayer

When your grandchildren live far away from you, prayer becomes even more important as a way to be involved in their lives. My cousin Justin Rice, who lives in Nashville, Tennessee, has seven grandchildren living in a variety of time zones—from Atlanta, Georgia, to Los Angeles, California, to Vancouver, Washington.

One year he was asked by his grandchildren what he would like for Christmas, and he told them that he would like coffee mugs with photos of all his grandchildren on the mugs.

These can be ordered online quite inexpensively. So his wish was granted, and that year he received seven coffee mugs, each with a photo of one of his grandchildren.

Since Justin had seven grandchildren, he then decided to name each day of the week after one of his grandkids. So Sunday became Hunter-day, Monday became Noah-day, Tuesday became Anna-day, and so forth. Justin let all of his grandkids know that every week—on their day—he would be drinking coffee from their mug in the morning and praying especially for them. Justin also took time during the day to make a phone call, send an email, or text a message to each grandchild on their day to let them know he remembered to pray for them that day. Needless to say, this is something his grandchildren look forward to each week, and they are well aware which day of the week is "their day."

You don't have to have seven grandchildren to do something like this. Even with one grandchild, you can set aside a day a week to be a special day when you intentionally take time to pray for them in earnest and remember them before the Lord. This might also be the day for your weekly phone call or text message so your grandchild knows that on that particular day you were thinking about and praying for him or her.

For Further Reflection and Action

1. How often do you pray for your grandchildren?
2. Paul prayed for specific blessings and behaviors on behalf of his "children" in Colossians. Which of these do you also pray for your grandchildren?
3. Write down each of your grandchildren's names and specific needs that each has. If you aren't sure what they are, contact your grandchildren and ask them, "How can I be praying for you?"

The Personal Connection

If you are a long-distance grandparent, there are numerous ways to stay connected with grandkids—using the U.S. mail, phones, computers, and the like. But all these modern conveniences—as wonderful as they are—really can't substitute for the best way to connect with our grandkids, which is to be with them in the flesh as often as possible. Intentional long-distance grandparents generally accept the fact that they are going to spend a lot of time on planes, trains, and automobiles. Or, they are going to have to find ways to encourage and/or make it possible for their grandkids to make the trip "over the river and through the woods" to grandma and grandpa's house themselves. This chapter offers a few practical ideas for making the most of the opportunities you have to connect with your grandchildren live and in person.

Create a Grandparenting Calendar

One of the reasons why some long-distance grandparents neglect to visit their grandkids is simply because of poor planning.

Life can get very busy, even for grandparents! If you don't plan to do something, it likely will not get done. So why not create a calendar especially with your grandchildren in mind? When are the best times to visit? Plan your visits well in advance so that your grandchildren (and their parents, of course) can get these dates on their calendars as well. Are there times when you would like your grandchildren to visit you? What about phone or video calls? Will you do these on a weekly, bi-weekly, or monthly basis?

Do you have your grandchildren's special events on your calendar? Birthdays or other special days in their lives? Are your grandchildren involved in sports or other activities with recitals, games, graduations, or performances? You will want to make sure to have all these things on your calendar so you can plan to attend if the distance isn't too great. The key here is to be intentional rather than haphazard in your grandparenting efforts. A little planning can go a long way toward bridging the long-distance gap with your grandkids.

Create a Grandparenting Budget

Likewise, a major problem for many long-distance grandparents is not having the financial resources necessary to stay connected with their grandchildren. You can pretty much take it to the bank that the farther away your grandchildren live from you, the more expensive it will be for you to stay in touch with them, especially if travel is involved. What you don't want to do is give your grandkids the leftovers of your budget. Chances are you will not have anything left. When that's the case, you will always find grandparenting to be an uncomfortable intrusion on your lifestyle rather than something you anticipate and plan in advance to do.

Sit down and add up how much you think it will cost to do everything that you want to do with your grandkids. You can probably make reasonable estimates to cover things such as air or ground travel, hotel costs, rental cars, gifts, amusement parks or other attractions, and other miscellaneous expenses. Depending on how far away your grandkids live and what you would like to do, the total amount could be quite significant. Of course, there are many free or very inexpensive things you can do with your grandkids, but if you have the means to spend money on your grandchildren, the best way to do it is to plan it into your budget well in advance.

One often overlooked budgetary item for long-distance grandparents is postage. If you are being intentional about staying connected with your grandchildren, you can spend a small fortune sending them letters and care packages. Grand-children love to receive gifts from their grandparents, and in many cases, the cost of shipping is greater than the gift itself!

While we're on the subject of budgeting, be on the lookout for special deals on travel from your favorite airline or from dis-count carriers like Spirit and Southwest. You can often sign up online to receive notifications when special fares are announced. Sometimes our kids let us know when they hear about special deals. These fares are usually available for less-busy travel days during the year, but if you are flexible and plan in advance, you can save a lot of money and go see your grandkids more often!

When You Go Visit Your Grandchildren

As I said earlier, the key here is to plan your visit in advance. Make sure that the time for your visit doesn't interfere (too much) with your grandchildren's (and their parents') normal daily responsibilities and routines. If they have work, school, or other activities that are important (and they most likely do), you will need to find something else to do during the day when they are busy. The best way to plan ahead is to try to match your visit with a break in your grandchildren's schedule—such as during their winter or spring break, over a holiday weekend, or during summer vacation.

Do a little research if you are not familiar with where they live. If your grandchildren live near tourist attractions, it might be fun to have them accompany you on a visit. Most people who live near tourist attractions rarely go there themselves. You can take your grandkids on day trips to visit parks, museums, and other interesting things nearby.

When you do visit your children and grandchildren, be sure to spend some individual time with your grandchildren away from their parents. I have found that you have to be intentional about this or you will spend all your time with their parents—which isn't a bad thing—but your grandchildren really do need some dedicated time with their grandparents. They will cherish those times because it tells them that they are loved and highly valued. Play some games with them, go for walks, or make a trip to the ice cream parlor. Don't use this time as an "information dump" when you try to force-feed them with Bible verses or spiritual truth. Just have some fun and look for opportunities to tell them how much you love them and how much God loves them too.

Remember that every grandchild is different. Some will eagerly look forward to your visits and want to spend all the time they have with you. Others—especially the older grandchildren—will not look forward to your visit so much. Don't take this personally, as it is normal and natural as children grow up and into lives of their own. They have other interests and they are quite good at compartmentalizing their lives so they can spend appropriate time with their family and then move on to other things—usually spending time with their friends or on social activities they enjoy. Don't expect all of your grandchildren to drop everything and spend all their time with you; it likely won't happen, and you will be disappointed. But if you plan ahead and include some fun activities, it's likely that your grandkids will look forward to your visit and do all they can to make your visit a memorable one.

After the Visit

Here's an idea that can extend your visit for a few hours—or even a few days! Leave little notes or small gifts to be found in their home after your departure. Better yet, hide them and call the grandkids later to give them clues to solve.

Or, leave a few wrapped gifts with your grandchildren's parents during your visit. Ask them to keep them stashed away and handy so they can be given to your grandchildren on special occasions, holidays, when they are sick, or other times when they need a little reminder that their grandparents are thinking about them.

Just You and the Grandkids

Here's a great way to do something nice for your adult children and also get some quality time with your grandkids. Send the parents away on a mini-vacation while you stay with the grandchildren at home. Some couples who have young children deny themselves the time they need to refresh their marriage with a romantic getaway or time alone to do something special together. I know grandparents who take the initiative to plan and finance occasional weekend trips for their adult children just so they can baby-sit the grandkids. It's definitely a win-win if you are able to do something like this.

When Your Grandchildren Come to Visit You

When you are a long-distance grandparent, it's always a special treat when the grandkids come to visit. Whether or not the visit includes their parents, you will want to make every visit a happy and memorable experience for the grandchildren. You'll want to spend some individual time with each grandchild if you possibly can. Many grandparents create living spaces especially for the grandchildren so they will be familiar with the home and look forward to their stay. If they have their own room (or even their own air mattress for the living room floor), a box of toys, games they can play, and other fun things to do while they are with you, so much the better.

Before the Visit

It's not just the visit with you that gets grandkids excited. It's counting down the days until the visit happens. If you do a little prep work ahead of time, you can leverage this excitement to make their visit even more special. Here are a few ideas:

- If you have in mind a few places you will go together during their visit, capture a few photos or videos of those sites and send them to the grandkids. This helps the grandkids picture themselves in those locations.
- Create a "Coming Attractions" calendar. Print out a blank calendar template and mark off the dates of the upcoming visit. Then, using words, pictures, or photos, fill in the dates with activities you plan for the visit. One terrific way to fill in the calendar is to mail it back and forth for several days prior to the visit. This way, both grandparents and grandchildren can have input into the agenda, and everyone gets a chance to become excited.
- Send a container with the exact number of pieces of your grandchild's favorite candy as days that are left until your next visit. Include instructions for your grandchild to eat one piece a day until you are together.

During the Visit

While the grandkids are visiting, you don't have to program every minute of the day, but it's good to know in advance what you are going to do with them. Sometimes just letting them rest, play by themselves, take naps, or watch TV is a completely acceptable activity. For one thing, you may not have the energy to keep them entertained all day. But if you can, there are plenty of options. Here are a few examples:

- Provide older grandchildren with a space of their own if possible.
- Learn and keep their bedtime routines. Their parents will appreciate it.
- Spend time with your grandchildren visiting places like the zoo, the park, and the library, but don't stop there. Make the visits memorable. Swing with him at the park or take your shoes off and wade through the water. Make s'mores with her at the beach or curl up with a book at the library.
- Put out the "welcome mat"—a special glass, fancy plate, pillow, blanket, chair, wading pool, tricycle/bicycle, sidewalk chalk, bubbles, etc.
- Have some items in your home that are just for their visits.
- Stock up on their favorite foods and snacks.
- Keep a "Grow Chart" for each grandchild and update it on each visit.
- Designate a "Place of Honor" for your grandchild, such as a special seat at the dinner table.
- Let your grandson or granddaughter help you build something. Grandchildren love to help their grandparents with projects, even if they wouldn't do this at home. I know one grandparent who built a very elaborate tree house in his backyard with the help of his grandkids. Of course

now the grandkids can't wait to come for a visit just so they can continue to work on (and play in!) their new tree house. Another grandparent purchased one of those do-it-yourself tool shed kits from the local Home Depot and put it all together one weekend when his grandson was visiting. Doing something together like this provides a wonderful opportunity to spend time together and also to teach your grandkids some valuable skills that will come in handy later on in life. They will never forget what they learn from you.

After the Visit

You can get some extra mileage from your grandchild's visit with you by tucking a special note or small gift in your grandchild's luggage to be found when he or she returns home.

You can also make a photo book or collage of pictures that you took while your grandchildren were visiting you. Ask your grandkids to write captions for the photos and send them back to you (or post them online). This is a great way to create some memories that will last a long time.

Camp Grammy and PawPaw

Here's another idea that many grandparents have found to be a great way to spend time with their grandkids (all at once!) and also give the grandkids a chance to be with their cousins. Plan a multiday "Camp Grammy and PawPaw" (or "Camp G&G," "Cousins Camp," or whatever you would like to call it) and invite all of your grandchildren to come to your house for several days of fun. Obviously a lot of advance planning will have to be done—to find a time when all the grandchildren are out of school and to make all the other arrangements—but it can definitely be worth it. Your "camp" can include all the accoutrements of a summer camp program with games, crafts,

Bible lessons, trips to parks and zoos, singing, good kid food, late-night movies, and even T-shirts. You don't have to do everything yourself unless you are willing and able. It's likely that some of the parents will be available to help out.

Meeting Half Way

As a way to create lasting memories for grandchildren, many families plan special family gatherings at a desirable location that is capable of housing everybody and providing plenty of fun things to do. You and your family may have a favorite place where you like to return on an annual (or occasional) basis, such as a campsite in the woods, a cabin on a lake, a condo on a beach, or even a cruise ship or amusement park where you can spend a few days together. This could take the form of a vacation or family reunion or the celebration of a holiday, birthday (yours!), or anniversary. Some grandparents like to call these kinds of family gatherings "cousin chaos" because they are usually noisy if the family is large. Sometimes these events are the only times your grandkids have to get to know their cousins, uncles, and aunts. And it's great for them to see how much you love them all as the patriarch or matriarch of the family.

Special Trips with Your Grandchildren

Another way to spend quality time with your grandchildren is to plan a special trip with them to a place that is meaningful or fun. Here are some examples:

Grand Camps

Christian "grand camps" are springing up all across the country. They are usually sponsored by a ministry organization or Christian camp and offer a summer camp experience for grandparents and their grandchildren together. They are usually held at a Christian camp that provides comfortable accommodations, food, outdoor activities, and a full-service program especially designed for creating a bond between grandparents and grandchildren. For more information, visit GrandCamps. org, a ministry of the Christian Grandparenting Network. There are other grand camps out there as well, so check them out and consider going to camp with one or two of your long-distance grandkids.

Mission Trips and Service

There are many churches and mission organizations sponsoring mission trips that are intergenerational (open to all ages). My local church in San Diego has for several years sponsored an intergenerational mission trip to Mexico that involves building a house for a family living in poverty and also conducting a VBS (Vacation Bible School) program for neighborhood children. It's a great way for parents and their children (or grandparents and their grandchildren) to have a life-changing experience together serving Christ.

You don't have to go to another country to participate in a mission and service, of course. There are lots of opportunities in your own community to volunteer and make a difference in the lives of other people. Not all mission projects are suitable for young children, but many are, and they can provide a wonderful way for you to pass along your faith and values to your grandchildren with your actions, not just your words.

Rites of Passage or Educational Trips

If you have the means to do so, you might want to plan an educational trip for each of your grandchildren when they reach a certain age. My cousin Justin takes each of his grandchildren on a trip to Washington, D.C., when they turn twelve years of age. This trip serves as a rite of passage for each of the grandchildren, who look forward to getting this special trip with grandma and grandpa. But they have to be old enough to travel on their own and appreciate their visit, so there's an age requirement before each grandchild can go. Of course, all the details have to be worked out long in advance and in cooperation with parents. The sky's the limit when it comes to ideas for trip itineraries. You might want to do an "ancestry tour" and show your grandkids where you grew up or where your family originally came from. If your ancestors emigrated from Ireland, for example, a trip to the Emerald Isle might be in order.

Moving Near the Grandkids

This is sometimes referred to as "chasing the grandkids" and it's not for the faint of heart. But many grandparents choose to do it, even multiple times.

In some cases, such a move may be necessary for you. If your children are in the position of providing care for you as you get older, it's hard for them to do that from a distance. And they are the ones who likely have to stay put. So they may invite you to move closer or even to move into their home if they have room for you. While this may create some hardship, it more often than not makes life easier for your children as well as for you.

In most cases, however, the decision to move closer to your children and grandchildren is optional and needs to be made by you with the best interests of your kids and grandkids at heart.

For some grandparents, the decision to move is a no-brainer. The reasons are clear: Life is short (and getting shorter all the time), and they don't want to miss out on spending time with their grandchildren! So even if it is difficult to pull up stakes and move to another part of the country, it may be worth it in the long run.

But a move is not without risks. One, of course, is that your children may have to relocate once again for work reasons and be forced to leave you behind a second or third time. That's where the phrase "chasing the grandkids" came from. So you have to ask yourself—is moving from place to place a good practical or financial decision? How many times will you have to do this? There's no question that the decision whether to be a nearby grandparent or one from afar takes a lot of thought and prayer.

Harriet Edleson, writing in the *New York Times*, offers this advice based on interviews with grandparents who have made the move to be near their grandkids:

- Consider the relationship you have with your adult child. No matter how good it is, figure out your boundaries and how you would develop your own life if you moved.
- Decide how you are going to spend your time in the new location. [One woman] found a part-time job and joined the local Chamber of Commerce so she was not always dependent on her family to use up her time and energy.
- Realize you may be leaving longtime friends and the support of a community. Think about how to establish new relationships. . . .
- Analyze the financial impact of moving. If you have more than one child and more than one grandchild, and want to relocate, compare the cost of living in each area with the cost where you are. If finances are not a big factor, you can move anywhere. If they are, make sure you figure out a budget before you put your home on the market.[1]

If you are seeking a lot more time with your grandchildren, a permanent move may not be necessary. Some grandparents live temporarily near their grandchildren in an RV park or at an extended-stay hotel. With some creative thinking, there may be other ways for you to close the distance between you and your grandchildren, at least for some of the time.

For Further Reflection and Action

1. How often do you get to see your grandkids? Is that enough?
2. When is the next time you plan to go visit your grandchildren? When is the next time they will come to visit you?
3. List three things that your grandchildren love to do with you when you are together.
4. Have you considered moving to be closer to your grandchildren? If so, what has prevented or discouraged you from doing that?

The Long-Distance Connection

For most long-distance grandparents, a lot of time can go by between visits with our grandchildren. You may only be able to see your grandchildren once or twice a year, or even less frequently than that. How can you have a relationship with your grandchildren when you never see them?

This chapter contains ideas that may help you make that long-distance connection between you and your grandchildren. Remember that they are here for you to consider and to try as you see fit. Not all of them will sound feasible or appropriate for you, which is perfectly okay. Some of them don't work for me either. But they are good ideas that have been very helpful to a good many grandparents who want to stay connected to their grandkids.

Snail Mail

Also known as the U.S. Postal Service, snail mail may be relatively slow but it's still something we can use very effectively as grandparents to stay in touch with our grandkids. Everyone loves to get something personal in the mail, and grandkids are no exception. Here are some ideas to get you started.

Write That Letter

Letters may be pretty old-school compared with email and text messages, but they are unrivaled for their personal touch. There is always something special about getting a handwritten letter. A few letter-writing tips:

- Use print, not cursive, when writing to young children, and keep the letter short and simple.
- Talk about personal and individual topics, not the weather.
- Write about things you enjoy or appreciate about your grandchild.
- Share your own interests and experiences.
- Share your faith without being preachy or too abstract. Give specific examples of how you have seen Christ at work in your life or in theirs.
- Use humor.
- Use a highlighter to draw attention to things you don't want your grandchild to miss.
- Include pictures you've drawn or cut out, photographs, or coloring pictures.
- Tuck small items in your letters from time to time. This could be something such as a stick of gum, a sheet of stickers, or a magnet.
- Attach stickers to emphasis a point, or put one next to your signature, on the envelope, or just for fun.
- Create your own personalized signature. Every time you send a letter to your grandchild, be sure to use a dot of that same perfume, attach that identical fuzzy sticker, or draw that smiley face on the envelope or next to your name. It

won't be long before your mail is immediately recognized and eagerly opened.

Postcard Blessings

Children love to get mail, so why not get in the habit of sending your grandkids a weekly postcard? It only takes a minute to dash off a quick note, and interesting postcards are easy to find. Aside from post offices and card shops, you can find cards decorated with local images at restaurants, hotels, tourist attractions, even the grocery store. You can also purchase a set of postcards with Bible verses on them from several online retailers. They are generally inexpensive, and postcard stamps are considerably less than regular first-class stamps for envelopes. So get creative and let your grandkids know what's going on in your life in twenty-five words or less. You can also add a special blessing over them to encourage them and put a smile on their face. They will love it and look forward to each one.

Incoming Mail

Here's a good way to get regular communication back from your grandchild. Send her a package of pre-addressed, pre-stamped postcards and ask her to mail one to you every week (perhaps on the same day of the week). You can ask her to give you specific information, such as "something fun I did this week" or "I felt close to God this week when . . ." or "My prayer request for this week is . . ." You could write those questions (or similar ones) on the cards or enclose a list of questions they can choose from each week.

And for those grandkids who are not as adept at writing, many arts and crafts stores sell watercolor postcards that can be sent along with a watercolor brush and paint sets so your grandchildren can send you their creations. Just ask mom and dad to help them send a postcard every week or two and you'll never run out of artwork to put on your refrigerator door. Sometimes the greatest barrier to sending mail is just not having the supplies you need. You can remedy this by sending the supplies and letting your grandchild know that you love getting those cards from her each week.

More Postcard Fun

How about sending your grandchild a series of postcards that communicate a message over time? Use the first card to ask a question, like "Where will we go on your birthday?" Then send the answer, one letter or clue to a card, such as: I, S, F, I, G, H, N. Your grandchild can unscramble them to discover the answer: FISHING. Be creative and make each postcard fun. Use colors and stickers to add pizzazz. You could also send your grandchild an album to hold all the postcards and share with their friends and family. This idea is also effective as a way to teach simple lessons from the Bible as well. For example, each postcard can include a letter or word that answers the question "What is your grandmother's favorite Bible verse?"

Mailing to Multiple Grandkids

If you have more than one grandchild at the same location, be careful when you are sending cards, letters, or gifts. Mailing them all on the same day is no guarantee that they will all arrive on the same day. To prevent disappointment, send them together in one package. You can still send them in individual envelopes, but mailing them together in one larger package will ensure that all your grandchildren receive their letters or gifts at the same time. That's a win-win.

Post a Puzzle

Instead of sending your grandchild a letter or picture, why not make it more interesting by sending them a personalized jigsaw puzzle? You can buy blank puzzles at hobby stores or online for under $1 in a variety of shapes and sizes. You can then write your letter on the puzzle or draw a picture. Many puzzles even come with envelopes or boxes for mailing. If you are able to spend a little more money, there are several online services that let you turn photos into puzzles as well (such as CreateJigsawPuzzles.com or Jigsaws.com). Puzzles vary by size and the number of pieces you choose, but they are always fun for kids to put together.

Mail a Kiss

Send a bag of Hershey's Kisses to your grandchild's parent. Include instructions that a "Kiss" be given to your grandchild each day with a message that the "Kiss" is from grandma or grandpa. This can also be done with a bag of Hershey's Hugs.

Something in Common

Your grandchild probably has a to-do list that is very different from yours: taking karate lessons, going to school, riding a bicycle, shooting hoops. Your to-do list might be: pruning the rose bushes, playing bridge, cleaning the garage, going to doctor appointments. You may not have a lot in common, so why not initiate a new activity you can share. Mail the directions (or, if possible, the supplies) for something you both can do and then follow up by mailing each other updates and photos. Gardening is a great suggestion. Some fast-growing seeds that small hands can manage are beans, lettuce, marigolds, morning glories (soak overnight and plant directly outdoors), and sunflowers. You can have contests: Whose plant is first to sprout or flower? Whose is tallest? You could also master a new skill together such as preparing simple recipes, trying science experiments, performing magic tricks, or building a bird feeder. Or you could read a book together or do a Bible study. Your goal is to have something in common so you will have something to talk about when you phone or write.

Flooding the Mailbox with Birthday Cards

Here's a novel idea for sending birthday cards to your grandchildren. Send an individual birthday card for every year of your grandchild's life. So, if your granddaughter is six, she will receive six cards from you, each with a different message. You'll make quite an impression on your grandchild by flooding her mailbox with creative and fun cards just for her. You could even enclose a dollar bill, sticker, or other special gift in each one. The cards don't have to be expensive. They can be homemade, so the only expenses are paper, envelopes, stamps, and time.

Quilting Across the Miles

Do you know how to make a quilt? Nineteenth-century American women were known for their ingenuity when it came to keeping the family warm and fashionable by making quilts of discarded fabric. Reinterpret their technique by rescuing your grandchild's receiving blankets and baby clothes from the dusty attic and transforming them into an heirloom patchwork quilt that tells your family's story. FreeQuilt.com features beginner patterns for inspiration. As your grandchildren get older, the squares can be made from camp and concert T-shirts and can be embroidered with significant dates and accomplishments. Take turns adding squares to the blanket by mailing it back and forth.

Undigital Photos

Send inexpensive plastic cameras to your grandchildren and include pre-addressed, stamped, padded envelopes for their easy return. Equipped with a camera, a child feels important and powerful and will gladly snap photos to share with Granny. When you ask your grandchildren to show you what their lives are like by taking pictures of their friends, pets, schools, or trips, you will surely get a response. Have parents mail the cameras back to you so you can get the film developed and share in their lives away from you. The next time the kids visit, you can look through the photo album together and talk about all the pictures together.

Speaking of Photos

Make sure your grandchildren's parents are armed with plenty of photos of you. One grandmother I know mounted her and her husband's enlarged photos on cardboard backing and asked the parents to show her grandchild the images whenever they talked on the phone!

Flat Grandpa

This idea is based on the Flat Stanley Project (FlatStanley Project.com) in which children send cutout paper dolls of "Flat Stanley" to another person and ask them to keep a journal and take pictures of Flat Stanley in interesting locations or doing interesting things. Why not send your grandchild a cutout paper doll of you (Flat Grandpa or Flat Grandma) and ask your grandchild to take the doll to some of his or her favorite places or on an adventure that you might really enjoy. He or she can then write down what happened in a journal and take pictures that can be sent back to you. If you can find a copy of the book *Flat Stanley* by Jeff Brown, send it along with the doll.

Money in the Mail

This may or may not be something you can do with any regularity, but it's almost guaranteed that your grandchildren will delight in receiving small gifts of money from time to time. It doesn't have to be a lot. Send money for the ice cream truck or a kiddy ride at the store. Or send a little more money for a back-to-school shopping day. Or send ten one dollar bills and instruct your grandchild to put one of them in the offering plate at Sunday school or church. The other nine can be saved or used for whatever they choose to spend it on.

Telephones and Text Messaging

Call Your Grandkids

Today's smartphones are used for almost everything except making phone calls. But talking on the phone is still a great way to connect with your grandchildren. Here are a few tips:

- Call each grandchild separately.
- Check with the child's parents. Be sure your calls do not interfere with family routines.
- Make sure your grandchildren know that they can call you anytime (within reason).
- Ask open-ended questions when talking with your grandchildren. That is, avoid questions that can simply be answered yes and no or you'll have a pretty short conversation.
- Listen. Pay close attention to what they are saying. Then respond by asking more questions to help you understand.
- Keep a pad and pencil by the phone and take notes as your grandchildren talk. Keeping track of the little details will show them that you really care. You can use this as a reference when you call next time.
- Find your own unique way to end each phone conversation. Ask them for prayer requests, and close with prayer or give them a blessing.

Text a Joke

Most grandchildren love to hear (and read) jokes and riddles. If your grandchild gets a text from you that reads "Knock knock," you will be sure to get one back very quickly, "Who's there?" Just be on the lookout for good ones and you'll find that jokes can be a fun way to cross the miles with smiles.

Text a Photo

Get in the habit of taking selfies when you are out and about and sending them via text message to your grandkids. They will love to see your face and know that you are thinking about them wherever you are.

Marco Polo

There is an app called Marco Polo that you can download on your smartphone and send instant video text messages to your grandkids. The kids love it because you can also add special effects and filter your voice in funny ways. For instance, you can add the "helium voice" effect and sound like Mickey Mouse. It's pretty hilarious, and hopefully it (or something like it) is still available by the time this book is published.

Bitmoji

Another fun thing to do with your smartphone is to create your own customized "emoji" or "avatar" that can be sent with text messages, emails, etc. Download the Bitmoji app and follow the directions. Your grandkids will love it.

Discuss a TV Show or Movie

Even though you are far away from your grandchildren, you probably get the same TV shows or have access to the same movies they watch. Why not agree to watch the same TV show or movie and then call or text each other when the movie is over to talk about it? Try to choose age-appropriate shows and movies that your grandchild would like to watch or find entertaining.

Technology

Your grandchildren are growing up in a world of rapid and constant change, and most of that change is taking place in the world of technology. Your grandchildren are likely part of the generation researchers are calling "iGen"—the first generation of kids to grow up with smartphones in their hands.[1] Today's kids spend more time every day online (connected to the Internet) than any previous generation, including millennials. Our grandchildren can hardly imagine a world without the Internet and all that it provides for them every day of their lives.

Just remember that the technology keeps changing. A commercial on TV recently pictured a child with her tablet (iPad, perhaps), and her mother asks, "What are you doing on your computer?" The girl's response: "What's a computer?" Some of our kids today don't even use the same language that we used about technology a few years ago. You don't have to keep up with all the latest gizmos and gadgets, but I would recommend that you not shut out your grandchildren by not making an effort to utilize the technology that is available and easy to learn. I know one grandpa who told his family, "Don't buy me anything that has a screen on it. I'll just throw it in the trash." What he was saying to his family was essentially, "I am not willing to spend any time or make any effort at all trying to understand your world or communicate with you."

So, at the risk of making this book obsolete by the time you have a chance to read it, I offer you a few ideas for using technology to stay connected with your iGen grandkids. For younger grandchildren, of course, you will need to work with their parents and get their permission to make contact over the Internet. They may also need to provide help as well as the hardware.

Email

Most of today's kids do not use email very much, if at all. They text and use social media platforms like Snapchat and Instagram to connect with their friends. Still, email has its place and can be used as a way to connect with your grandchildren if they have their own email accounts set up. Even if they don't, you can email messages to your grandkids by sending them to their parents and putting "An email for (grandchild's name)" in the subject line. The nice thing about emails is that they are quick, easy, and cheap. And email is a very adult thing to do, which has appeal for some kids. Most of us use email a lot to communicate with friends and coworkers, so using email seems rather grown-up for some of our grandchildren.

If your grandchildren like to get email, set up a routine. Email your grandchild once a day or once a week. Email before leaving for work or going to bed. Don't expect them to reply to every email, but let them know that you are thinking about them, praying for them, and love them very much. You can have some fun with your emails by sending messages in a secret code or letter scrambles. You can also include attachments—coloring pages, photos (perhaps in a PowerPoint program), recordings, or puzzles to solve. Use an Internet crossword puzzle program to make a personalized crossword for your grandchild. You can use memories, favorite activities, and information about other family members as clues. You can also play a game of 20 Questions by email, which keeps the conversation going for days or even weeks. The continuous back-and-forth helps keep the lines of communication open.

Audio Recordings as Email Attachments

If your computer or device has an app that allows you to make voice recordings and save them in an MP3 format, you can send them as email attachments. You can also send them via text message or other programs as well. Why not record yourself reading a book or selections from the Bible for your grandchildren and then send the recording by email. Mail a copy of the book along with the recording so your grandchild can follow along as you read. You can even add the "beep" to indicate page turns and add comments as you read.

Videoconferencing

That's the term commonly used to describe face-to-face conversations on your personal computer, laptop, tablet, phone, or other screen. Welcome to the future! It wasn't too long ago when having video conversations across hundreds or thousands of miles was only possible in science-fiction movies. It's truly amazing how technology has in recent years made it possible for us to have live video conversations at any time, anywhere, in real time. Programs like Skype, Google Hangouts, Zoom, Appear.in, FaceTime, and others are increasingly easy to use. If you are not familiar with how to use them, I would recommend that you learn as soon as possible. If you are not computer savvy (and there are many in my generation who are not), have someone else help you get a simple setup so you can take advantage of this truly wonderful way to connect with your grandchildren.

As I mentioned, there are many videoconferencing programs available right now, and there likely will be even more by the time you read this book. Technology changes very quickly. Skype and FaceTime are two of the most popular mainly because they come pre-installed on many devices. If your grandchildren have iPhones, FaceTime is probably what they are most familiar with. But there are other good programs as well, and most have free versions that are usually sufficient for connecting with your grandchildren.

I personally prefer Zoom because it's easy to use and I like the way it displays everyone on the screen who is on the call. My wife and I try to connect with our entire family using Zoom on a regular schedule, which involves at least four locations from San Diego to Seattle. I can set up a meeting and then send the link to everyone by email. They click on the link at the appropriate time, and voila!—we are all on the call together. We can see each other on the screen and we can talk to each other as if we are all in the same room. And in a way, we are. You can also set up Zoom calls automatically, so that you can connect on a weekly, bi-weekly or monthly basis. Appear.in is a similar program that gets good reviews.

If your grandchildren have their own computers or tablets, schedule a regular weekly or bi-weekly video call with them. Our calls usually include the parents, and we have family video calls with all the kids and grandkids participating. While that's a great time to catch up with each other, it's not the best time to have more personal conversations. To do that, it's better to schedule these calls with each grandchild individually. Just as with personal visits, it's always a good idea to spend some one-on-one time with your grandchildren.

It's smart to have a few questions prepared ahead of time that you can ask your grandkids or other conversation starters. The nice thing about video is that you can add a little "show and tell" to the conversation. To liven things up, wear a costume or make funny faces. If you are reading a book together, you can turn the pages and show illustrations. The bonus of being able to see as well as hear opens up all kinds of possibilities.

I know grandparents who teach piano lessons to their grandchildren using FaceTime. They can set their iPads on the music holders and see each other's fingers on the piano keys. This allows them to watch and hear at the same time. I know grandparents who tutor their grandchildren in subjects such as math and history—using Skype. There are probably many things you can teach your grandchildren even though you are far away from them. The technology allows you to do that, so why not take advantage of it?

Long-Distance Doodling

If your grandchild has access to a computer or tablet with a Google email account (Gmail), there's a great way to do some doodling or coloring together online. Check out the Scoot & Doodle app on Google Hangouts. If you aren't sure how to access or use Google Hangouts, there are numerous instruction guides and tutorials available online, and if your grandchild is computer savvy, he or she can probably help you get things set up on your computer. It's relatively easy to use. Scoot & Doodle is a kind of white board that you and your grandchild can draw on, even simultaneously. You can create drawings together or use it for doing homework, such as solving math problems. You can use it to teach lessons or illustrate Bible stories, or you can simply play tic-tac-toe, hangman, or any other game that involves paper and pencil. If your grandchild enjoys this kind of activity, make it a weekly appointment and enjoy the time together. Google Hangouts also allows you to video chat and talk to each other while you are online, so it's similar in that regard to Skype, Zoom, and other videoconferencing apps.

Personalized Books

There are several websites like PutMeIntheStory.com and MyFairyTaleBooks.com that allow you to create and publish a children's book customized with the name of your grandchild in the story, and sometimes you can put yourself in the story too. These websites offer dozens of familiar stories such as Mother Goose rhymes and popular cartoon characters, but there are a few books with a Christian message too. For example, one of the stories is titled *God Loves* ____(insert name of child), and it helps children realize that they are children of God and loved by Him. There are other stories appropriate for holidays, birthdays, etc., and they make special gifts for children who live far away from you. Next time you visit, you can read the story together—or have the child read the story to you, on the phone or by videoconference.

Play Games Online

There are quite a few classic games you can play online with your grandchild. Games like Scrabble, chess, checkers, and Monopoly can be accessed on websites such as Pogo.com. Most allow you to play these games against players in other cities, states, and even other countries. Of course, parents will need to supervise and give their approval. Some websites are free, while others require a paid membership. If your grandkids are experienced game players, they can show you how it's done.

Mad Libs Online

Speaking of games, the old game of Mad Libs is always popular with kids. There are several Mad Libs websites that allow you to enter the missing words (noun, verb, adjective, etc.) and then they output a funny story. You might have your grandchild provide the words; then you could read back the story and share the laughs.

Write a Story Together

There are a number of free online applications such as Google Docs that allow you to collaborate with others on documents of various kinds. These applications are used frequently in businesses with offices all over the world. The documents are posted online and anyone who is part of the group can download and edit or add content to them. One way to use this application with your grandchildren is to collaborate on writing a story. Every day (or every week), you or your grandchild can add a new line, paragraph, or chapter to the story—back and forth—until it comes to a climax and it's time to end. Try to incorporate a Christian world view into your story and it will be a fun and creative way to teach your grandchild about your faith and values.

Cloud File Sharing

Dropbox is one of many file-sharing services that allow you to store digital photos, videos, and other documents "in the cloud." A free version is available, or you can pay to get a premium membership that provides a lot more storage space and other options. Either way, you can create a file (name it whatever you like) and "share it" with your grandchildren. Use that file to store family photos and other things you would like your grandkids to see. If they have their own Dropbox account, they will be able to download photos from that file or upload their own. This is an alternative way (and an easier one for some) to share photos and other digital documents, rather than attaching them to emails or sending by text message.

Family History Videos

Not sure what to do with all those old slides and photos you have collected over the years? Why not produce a family history for your grandchildren on video—not a difficult process these days. There are many computer programs that can convert your photos into a video presentation with a soundtrack. If you aren't familiar with the technology, ask one of your grandkids for help. Once you know how it's done, choose the photos and then record your narration of the video with comments to help your grandchildren understand what they are seeing. You can also add a musical soundtrack from the time period involved. This is another great way to leave your memories and heritage with your grandchildren while you can.

Use that Video Camera

Most of us are able now to make videos easily with just our cell phones. But maybe you have a more elaborate setup and know how to use it. Here are a few more ideas for using video:

- Instead of writing a letter, record one.
- Record "A Day in the Life of Grandma/Grandpa."
- For very young grandchildren, videotape yourself playing peekaboo.
- Make a music video featuring yourself singing age-appropriate songs for your grandchild.
- Create a video tour of your home.
- Prepare your grandchild for an upcoming visit by recording places they'll see with you.
- Dramatize one of your grandchild's favorite stories featuring yourself in the lead role.
- Record yourself as you make a favorite recipe. Then send a sample of the treat along with the video.
- Have someone else record you and your spouse as you send a unique greeting together for a special occasion in the life of your grandchild, such as a birthday, recital, or tournament game.
- Ask your grandchild to record a special event he is participating in and send it to you.

Step It Up

If both your grandchild and you own Fitbits or other step-tracking devices, hold daily or weekly competitions.

Fantasy Sports Leagues

Here's one for grandpas (and grandmas too) who are into professional sports. If you have grandchildren who like sports, why not ignite a friendly rivalry by inviting them to join you in a fantasy sports league? There are numerous online fantasy leagues that don't involve money or gambling. And you'll quickly discover that age does not always give you an advantage. Fantasy sports leagues can keep you connected with your grandchild every week throughout the season, and one of you will end up with the family bragging rights for the rest of the year. Of course, you'll want to make sure that mom and dad give this their okay and supervise.

Teach Morse Code

Teach your grandchildren Morse code. Children love secrecy, and they'll want to teach their friends after they learn. This could be done via email with simple dots and dashes, such as "...---..." to indicate SOS. Note how educational this activity is too! And when two people share a secret (or a code), a strong bond develops.

Bird-Watching Challenge

If you or your grandchild enjoy the outdoors, try doing a little online bird watching together. You will each need a notebook, pen, binoculars, and a camera as you explore your respective neighborhoods in search of birds. Make notes on those you see and use field guides to identify them. Exchange photos online. During migratory seasons, this could be especially interesting. And the search really turns into a bonding activity when your grandchildren spot a new bird and get excited about it. Of course, you'll return the enthusiasm in kind!

Weekly News from Grandma and Grandpa

One way to stay in touch with your grandchildren is to create a weekly "news report" from your location and send it by email to them. I have a good friend who is a missionary in Belize. He posts regular "This Day in Belize" articles on Facebook as a way to stay in touch with his family and supporters. Since he is an excellent photographer, he always posts an interesting photo along with commentary that includes insights from Scripture or other observations from his Christian world view. Something like this could be done for your grandchildren to help them know what you are doing each week and how you see God at work in your everyday life.

A Few Miscellaneous Ideas

Put Grandkid Reminders All Over Your Home

After all, that's what refrigerator doors are for. Ask your grandchildren (or their parents) to send you some of their artwork or recent photos so you can put them on display in your home. Doing so will remind you every day to pray for your grandchildren and to stay in touch. It will also let your grandchildren know how important they are to you when they visit.

Open an Education Savings Account

There are various education savings plans (such as a Coverdell Education Savings Account or a 529 plan) that allow you to contribute money toward your grandchildren's education. These accounts that you open actually belong to the grandchild. You can oversee them and invest in financial instruments that provide growth over time. When the money is withdrawn for educational purposes (usually college), the money is tax-free to you and your grandchild. If you are able, set up an account for your grandchild, and as they get older, let them see how their money is invested. If you have the money in the stock market, you can take this opportunity to teach your grandchild about investing wisely and in a way that reflects your Christian values. They can watch their account change as the stock market goes up and down. This can be a good way to teach your grandchildren about stewardship, decision-making, patience, and much more.

Life's Little Instruction Book

You've probably seen those little books containing wise sayings and life lessons that are sold in bookstores and gift shops. Why not write your own? What are the most important "lessons to live by" that you have collected over the years? These could be sayings from your own parents or grandparents, or Bible verses that have special meaning to you. Put them all together and create your own book. Call it *Grandma's Little Life Lessons Book*, or something along those lines. You can write down your life lessons in a blank book, or you could have the book published by one of those online photo book websites. They often offer smaller books (for baby photos, etc.), which can include photos and captions. Pages can also include just text. A book with your favorite life lessons could become a very special treasure for your grandchild.

Your Family History Book

One of the best gifts you can give your grandchildren is a history of your family—which is also the history of their family. Write a short—or long—family history. Be sure to tell funny stories about your children (the parents of your grandchildren), your parents, your grandparents, and what life was like when you were their age. Tell about your family traditions growing up and what they meant to you. If possible, include photos and other mementos. Frame an old map, the deed to the family farm, a special letter, or a birth certificate. And of course take this opportunity to share with your grandchildren how you came to know Christ and what your faith has meant to you over the years.

For Further Reflection and Action

1. How often do you make contact with your grandchildren? How often do they contact you?
2. What is your grandchild's favorite way to connect?
3. After reading the ideas in this chapter, which ones seem like good possibilities for you and your grandkids? How can you begin implementing these ideas right away?

6

Holidays and Special Occasions

Every calendar year provides regular occasions for you to reach out to your grandchildren. There's a good chance they will be celebrating these holidays anyway, so take advantage of these occasions and include your grandchildren in your annual holiday planning.

New Year's

A New Year's Blessing

Call your grandchild on New Year's Eve and give them a special blessing for the new year. The Aaronic blessing from Numbers 6:24–26 would certainly be appropriate:

(Grandchild's name), as you begin this brand-new year, may "the Lord bless you and keep you; the Lord make his face shine upon you and be gracious to you; the Lord turn his face toward you and give you peace."

Or, you can offer them a special Bible verse or two for the new year:

Brothers and sisters, I do not consider myself yet to have taken hold of it. But one thing I do: Forgetting what is behind and straining toward what is ahead, I press on toward the goal to win the prize for which God has called me heavenward in Christ Jesus.

Philippians 3:13–14

"For I know the plans that I have for you," declares the Lord, "plans for welfare and not for calamity to give you a future and a hope."

Jeremiah 29:11 NASB

If you do this at midnight, you'll want to be sure to call your grandchild's parents ahead of time and make sure this is okay.

New Year's Party in a Box

Mail your grandchild a "party in a box" with balloons, noise-makers, streamers, confetti, and other ways to bring in the new year. Again, make sure the parents are okay with this.

Start a Devotional

The first of January would be a good time to start a year-long devotional series with one of your older grandchildren. If you have a devotional book or guide you can both follow, that makes it easy to do.

Valentine's Day

Send Valentines!

Of course, Valentine's Day is a great opportunity for you to express your love to your grandchildren. Mail Valentine cards to each of them. Be sure to mail them early enough that they will arrive on time. Note: If you are mailing to multiple children in the same family and wish for each one to receive his or her own piece of mail, prepare an individual envelope for each child but place them all in one larger envelope. This way all the mail will arrive on the same day, ensuring that no one feels left out.

Send a Whole Box Full of Valentines

Check with parents first to make sure they haven't already purchased Valentines for their kids. If they haven't you can buy dozens of inexpensive Valentine cards (with envelopes) and mail them to your grandkids for them to address and send to their classmates, relatives, and friends.

Send a Gift Box

Grandchildren always love receiving gifts. How about sending chocolate hearts or one of those giant chocolate kisses, or you could send flowers, cookies, or balloons, Or, instead of filling a box with candy, fill it with coloring books and crayons, reading books, small games, or other non-edible treats.

Send a "Heart Attack"

Cut out a dozen or so construction-paper hearts. Write on each of them something you admire or appreciate about your grandchild. Then mail them all together in an envelope addressed to your grandchild. Mention that you are sending them a "heart attack."

Send a Personalized Valentine's Day Shirt

There are several websites that print personalized messages on shirts, such as "My Grandma and Grandpa Love Me." You can order shirts with your particular "grandparent name" on them (like "Nana" or "Bubba") and they will be shipped directly to your grandchild. Google "Valentine's Day gifts for kids" and you'll find them.

Presidents' Day

Presidents' Day would be a good time to share with your grandchildren memories of all the presidents you have lived under during your lifetime. Who was the first president you remember as a child? Harry Truman, Dwight Eisenhower, John Kennedy? Most of our grandchildren only hear about these people from their history lessons. You have firsthand knowledge and personal impressions of these presidents as well as their policies—good and bad.

Easter

Easter is a wonderful holiday to celebrate with your family. At our home in Southern California we usually have nice weather, so for more than twenty-five years we held a big party for friends and family in our backyard that included lots of good food (a potluck), live music, an Easter egg hunt for the kids, and lots of fun. We wanted our children and grandchildren to know that Easter is about more than the Easter bunny and wearing nice clothes to church. The death and resurrection of Jesus is the centerpiece of our faith, the heart of the Gospel. So we tried to celebrate it as a family even more than Christmas! Now that our children and grandchildren have moved away, how can we celebrate long-distance?

Resurrection Eggs

One way is to send your grandchildren a set of Resurrection Eggs, which you can purchase online or at your local Hobby

84

Lobby. Or, to make them more meaningful for your grand-children, you can create them yourself. Resurrection Eggs have grown in popularity over the last few years and basically are a set of twelve plastic eggs that each contain a Bible verse and an object to illustrate the verse. When opened in order, the eggs tell the story of Christ's death and resurrection.

Typically, these are the contents of the twelve eggs:

1. A tiny plastic donkey (or you can make one out of felt)— Jesus rode to Jerusalem on a donkey (Matthew 21:1–11). You can buy tiny animals in toy stores or craft shops.

2. A tiny perfume bottle or piece of cotton soaked in perfume— Mary poured perfume on Jesus' feet (John 12:2–8).

3. A tiny loaf of bread, dinner plate, or fork—the Last Supper (Matthew 26:17–19).

4. Three pieces of silver (three nickels, dimes, or quarters would be great)—Judas betrayed Jesus (Matthew 27:3).

5. A cross (you can make one out of twigs or toothpicks and some dental floss to tie them together, with a spot of glue)—Jesus carried His cross to the site of the crucifixion (John 19:17).

6. A thorn or two from a rose bush, or a little toy crown with a thorn—Jesus crowned king of the Jews (John 19:2–3; Mark 15:17–18).

7. A pair of dice—The soldiers cast lots for Jesus' garment (John 19:23–24).

8. A nail—Jesus was nailed to the cross (John 20:25–29).

9. A sponge—They give Jesus a sponge soaked in vinegar to drink (John 19:28–30).

10. Spices (whole cloves are small and fragrant)—Jesus' body is prepared for burial (John 19:40).

11. A stone—They covered the entrance to Jesus' tomb with a large stone (Matthew 27:59–60).

12. Nothing (empty)—The tomb was empty. He has risen (Matthew 28:6)!

Since there are twelve eggs, you can put them in a regular egg carton (which can also be decorated), or you could put them in an Easter basket. Put a number on each egg, one through twelve. Send the eggs to your grandchildren at least two weeks before Easter. The idea is to open one each day on the twelve days leading up to Easter. If your grandchild cannot read, then ask mom or dad to read the verse and explain the symbol that is contained in each egg. Or, you could call your grandchild each day and read it with her on the phone.

April Fools' Day

Prank Your Grandkids

Find a good joke to play on your grandkids. For example, tell them you are sending them a box of brownies. Then send them a box with several brown construction paper *E*s in it. Or send them a package labeled "Donut Seeds"—which are actually Cheerios. It's possible to have some April Fools' Day fun even when you are far apart!

Do Something Silly

Put on some ridiculous makeup or clothing, then call your grandkids on FaceTime or Zoom (so they can see you) and ask them what they think. Or, if you are familiar with those face-swapping apps that are available (Snapchat, for example), send your grandchild a fun photo of yourself in a crazy pose (maybe with your face posed with a celebrity). Or put yourself in one of those JibJab animations and email it to them. This is a good day for your grandkids to see that you have a sense of humor and don't take yourself too seriously.

Mother's Day or Father's Day

Mom and Dad Scrapbook

Send your grandchild some old photos of their mom or dad on Mother's Day or Father's Day, or send other artifacts from their parent's childhood.

Coach Your Grandkids to Be Thoughtful

Encourage your grandkids by phone or video chat to do something special for mom and dad on their special days. Let your grandkids know that it's their job (not their parents') to make Mother's Day or Father's Day special. Homemade gifts are always best. Here are some ideas you can offer:

- Color a picture for mom.
- Purchase her favorite candy bar. Every mom needs a little chocolate!
- Give mom a "one hour of uninterrupted time" certificate—which means that the grandkids will not interrupt her during that special hour of personal time.
- Give mom a "no talking back certificate" good for one day.
- For dad, make a personalized T-shirt or baseball cap.
- How about giving dad a stack of "free chore" cards that he can redeem at any time—and of course the chore will be done!

Mothers-Fathers (Parents) Day

Here's one we used to do with youth groups. On the calendar, find the day that falls exactly halfway between Mother's Day and Father's Day. It usually falls on a Wednesday. Have your grandkids do something special to honor their parents on that day—maybe giving them extra hugs, preparing the evening meal, or providing a special dessert.

Graduation Day

If one or more of your grandkids is graduating (from grade school, middle school, high school, college, etc.), this is a great time to make a trip to witness the important occasion. As for gifts, most students prefer receiving a cash gift rather than stuff. This is especially true for high school and college grads who are likely incurring a lot more expenses as they move on up to the next phase of their lives.

Fourth of July (Independence Day)

If you can't attend a fireworks display on the Fourth with your grandkids, take a cell phone video of one and send it via text message to your grandkids. Or . . .

Fly That Flag

How about displaying an American flag at your home in honor of your grandchildren? Or maybe several flags, one for each.

Bike Flags

Send small flags and streamers your grandkids can use to decorate their bicycles.

Share a Favorite Memory

Send your grandchild a favorite memory of a Fourth of July celebration from your childhood. Maybe you have a story about how you served in the armed forces, or immigrated to America, or climbed the Statue of Liberty. Maybe you have some old pictures you can share.

Back to School

Long-distance grandparents can help their grandkids get ready for school by sending them a care package of school supplies, or by providing a gift card to their favorite clothing store so they can look sharp on their first day back at school.

Tell your grandkids about your school days. Perhaps you could have someone interview you and send a video to your grandkids with your responses to questions like these:

- How did you get to school? (Did you have to walk miles, in the snow, uphill both ways?)
- Did you take your lunch? What kind of foods did you take? Did you have a lunch box?
- How big was your school?
- What were your teachers like? Who was your favorite?
- What kind of desks did you have?
- What kind of playground activities were your favorite?
- What kind of grades did you get? What was your favorite subject?
- Did you ever get into trouble?
- Who were your best friends?
- Was peer pressure a problem for you back then?
- Were you a Christian at school? Was it easy or hard to be a Christian at school?

Labor Day

Labor Day in the USA is not only the official end of summer but a celebration of the working class. This might be a good time to share with your grandkids something from your working days (if you are retired) to let them learn more about what you did for a living. If you know what your grandchildren are considering for their future careers, ask them questions about their future and give them all the encouragement and advice you can.

Grandparents Day

Grandparents Day in the U.S. is on the first Sunday after Labor Day. If your grandkids are unaware of the holiday, you might remind them and set up a phone or video call!

Halloween

If your family enjoys celebrating Halloween, find a silly costume and take photos or a video of yourself that you can send your grandkids. They will love seeing you dressed up as a superhero or cartoon character. Here are some other ideas:

- Mail fall decorations for your grandchild's room.
- Make or buy your grandkids costumes for Halloween.
- Send money for your grandchild to buy their own pumpkin.
- Ask for a video of their pumpkin-carving escapades.
- Mail a box of treats. Chances are they already got plenty of candy, so choose mostly nonedible items.

If you have an opportunity to talk with your grandchildren about Halloween, let them know the origins of the holiday—which are both pagan and Christian. You may need to do a little research to familiarize yourself with the history of Halloween. If your family has chosen to opt out of the holiday, let your grand-children know why. If you do celebrate Halloween, encourage your grandkids to remember that for Christians the day is not about devils and witchcraft (which are closely associated with the pagan view) but rather about remembering the lives of saints and heroes of the faith (which is the Christian view). October 31 is also the day when we remember and celebrate the Protestant Reformation.

Thanksgiving

Thanksgiving is of course a great time to get the family together. Perhaps this year will be a good year to organize a family reunion around the Thanksgiving dinner table. Remember to make it a special time for the children as well as all the grown-ups. If possible, include grandkids around the dining room table rather than sending them off to the "children's table."

Here are some other ideas you might want to try:

- Send each of your grandchildren a blank journal about a month prior to Thanksgiving. Ask them to list or draw in the journal something they are thankful for each day. These can be shared on Thanksgiving Day.
- Mail construction paper, cutouts, and other embellishments to your grandchildren so they can make their own Thanksgiving dinner placemats.
- Teach your grandchildren to draw a turkey by tracing their hand.

Christmas

It's the most wonderful time of the year, as the song goes, and the holiday season offers many ways to connect with your grandchildren across the miles. Of course, grandchildren always look forward to receiving Christmas presents from their grandparents. If you are like most grandparents, you have probably been shopping all year and stashing Christmas presents in a closet in the back bedroom. If you haven't done your Christmas shopping yet, here are a few tips:

- Think smaller gifts. The increased costs of postage and packaging make sending larger gifts very expensive. Consider gift cards to favorite stores.
- Or, send a check to mom and dad and ask them to shop for the grandkids. The upside of this is that the grandkids get what they want. The downside is you don't feel very involved.
- Give a family keepsake. This is an especially good idea for older grandkids—to give them something that you have owned and that has special meaning to you.
- It's okay to ask your grandchildren for their Christmas wish list. You can let their parents know which items you are going to purchase so they don't duplicate them.
- There are many ways to purchase Christmas gifts online now, such as with Amazon.com. You can have gifts sent directly to the child at their home address. Most of these services will gift wrap items for you, and you can enclose a note.
- Be sure to do your shopping and mailing early in the month so your gifts will arrive on time.
- Consider giving a gift in your grandchild's name to a mission organization such as Compassion International or World Vision. They have ways to provide gifts of food, clothing, farm animals, water wells, and other essentials to people all over the world living in poverty.

And some other ideas:

- Celebrate Advent with your grandchildren or the twelve days of Christmas by sending them Bible verses to read each day, counting down the days until Christmas.

- Begin a new tradition. Send/make each grandchild a specially chosen ornament for the family Christmas tree each year. Ask them to make one for you as well.
- Hang a stocking in your home for each of your grandchildren.
- Send cookies baked by grandma (or grandpa). Or, mail a box of cookie baking ingredients to your grandchild.
- Send them a gingerbread-house kit (available at many craft, department, and discount stores).
- Provide a small Christmas tree for each grandchild's room. Allow them to decorate it as they wish, or choose a theme appropriate for your grandchild's age.
- Make up new words to old Christmas songs. Record them on video and send them to your grandchildren.
- Make a JibJab Christmas card video for your grandkids. (Visit JibJab.com for more information.)
- On Christmas Eve (or some other agreed-upon time), read the Christmas story to your grandchildren via videoconference or speakerphone.
- Share in your grandchildren's Christmas morning joy via FaceTime or Skype.

Birthdays

Of course, you don't want to forget your grandchild's birthday. Put the birth dates of all your grandchildren on your annual calendar—better yet, put reminders on your calendar a week or two before their birthdays so you will remember to send those cards and gifts in plenty of time. Here are a few other ideas:

- Personalize birthday cards by attaching a photo of your grandchild's head to the card.

- Call after your grandchild's birthday party to get the scoop firsthand.
- Send a "birthday in a box." Buy party hats, balloons, decorations, gifts, and anything else your family traditionally uses for birthday celebrations. Box up the items and mail them to your grandchild.

Other Special Days

Perhaps you or your family have special days during the year that you can put on your calendar as good days to connect and celebrate—even from a distance. If you know the day that your grandchild was baptized or dedicated to Christ or their parents' wedding anniversary, these are days to celebrate. Sometimes a simple phone call letting your grandchild know that you are thinking about him or her on this special day is a good way to show that you love them.

For Further Reflection and Action

1. Which holidays are your favorites?
2. Do you have memories of celebrating holidays as a child with your parents and grandparents? What did you do?
3. What family traditions or celebrations would you like to pass along to your grandchildren?
4. The next time you visit your favorite shopping destination, keep your eyes open for interesting seasonal items you could use to bless your grandchildren this year. Most retailers display these items well in advance of the holidays, so let them be a reminder to you that an opportunity to connect with your grandchildren may be right there on the store shelf!

7

Connecting with Your Young Adult Grandkids

When Your Grandkids Are Away at College

So you went to your grandson's or granddaughter's high school graduation ceremony, and just like that, they disappeared—they went off to college! Every year some eleven million families wave good-bye to college-bound children. You have spent eighteen years of your life (and all of your grandchild's life) being an important caregiver and confidant, and now as they move off to those ivy-covered halls, you may be wondering if your grandparenting days are over.

Well, not so fast. Ask almost any college counselor and they will tell you that grandparents are highly revered by college students as pillars of wisdom and love that can't be equaled anywhere else. If anything, the perceived value of a grandparent goes up, not down, when kids go away to college. There still are important roles for you to play in the life of your college-bound grandchild.

One of those roles is to affirm your grandchild's emerging adulthood. This can be an exciting and somewhat conflicting time for a college-age grandchild who's living independently for the first time. Your grandson will confidently tell you he's an adult. His parents, however, will claim he's still a child. Parents sometimes have a hard time thinking of their children as young adults. They remember times (recently) when he forgot to fill the gas tank, hand in a homework assignment, take the garbage out—or eat breakfast. So parents are prone to become "helicopter parents" who hover over their child, even when he is away at college trying to figure out what it means to be all grown up. As a grandparent, it will be easier for you to recognize that your grandchild is both an emerging adult and still (in some ways) a naïve child with a lot of growing up to do. The challenge for grandparents is knowing when to treat a grandchild as an adult and when to cater to their childlike insecurities.

The ticket to keeping strong ties with your grandchild is maintaining open lines of communication. Nowadays, there's no shortage of communication methods available for reaching out to your older grandchildren. Emailing and texting are probably the best ways to stay in touch. These messages are likely to generate the fastest response from a grandchild, but a good old-fashioned phone call can work as well. If you can find out what your grandchild's daily schedule is (when she is in class, etc.), then you will know the best time to call.

When you do call or text, be sure to ask questions and learn all you can about your grandchild's new interests. Students are trying to transition into being adults, getting up on their own, figuring out meals, navigating a new town, making new friends, and dealing with roommates. They are also dealing with huge life questions, such as "Who am I?" and "What am I going to do for the rest of my life?" Grandparents can often be great sounding boards, if we are willing to ask questions and be good listeners. We can encourage grandchildren at each step of their journey and let them know that we are proud of them and are praying for them on a regular basis.

And speaking of prayer, here's a prayer list:

- Pray that they will be disciplined in their study habits.
- Pray that they will have alert minds.
- Pray for their health and safety.
- Pray that they will have wisdom regarding sleep, study, and eating habits.
- Pray that they will make good friends.
- Pray that they will be courageous and strong in their faith.
- Pray that they will become part of a faith community on campus where they can grow in their faith.

Even though your grandchildren are becoming young adults, they will still enjoy thoughtful reminders of their childhood. You can use the good old U.S. Mail to send postcards, handwritten letters, a little extra spending money, and various forms of memorabilia to your grandson or granddaughter on a regular basis. College students love to get care packages from home, and to get a ziplock bag of grandma's best cookies is about as good as it gets!

When college students come home for a visit, don't expect them to always have you high on their list of people to visit. The days of parents dictating, "Call your grandma," "Visit your grandpa," are over. When they do make the occasional weekend trip home, college students usually have busy schedules, cramming in visits with friends, parents, and other family members. As a grandparent, you may feel a little left out of this equation. Rather than waiting around pining for a visit, reach out to your grandchildren just as you would with any other adult friend. Invite them over or find out a good time when you can spend some time with them while they are home.

You can stay connected with your college-student grandchild in many ways. Just remember that your value goes up, not down, when your grandkids become young adults. If you have had an open and warm relationship with your grandchildren in the past, you will likely have many opportunities to become a source of great comfort, encouragement, and influence in their lives while they are away at college.

When Your Grandkids Are in the Military

If you have a grandchild who enlisted in the military, they will certainly appreciate hearing from you as frequently as possible—especially while they are in basic training. Since phone calls, packages, newspapers, and magazines are usually not allowed during the early part of training camp, here are a few ways you can connect:

- Write letters every day. Even if you don't have a lot to write about, your military grandchild will love to hear about the mundane things that are going on in your life. Letters don't have to be long. Some branches of the service make recruits do fifty push-ups for every letter they receive, but your grandchild would rather do the push-ups than not get a letter from home. Take comfort that you are just helping your grandchild build muscle! If you can't mail your letters daily, send two or three letters together in one envelope. Make your letters and notes as encouraging as possible. Add blessings for them and uplifting verses of Scripture to help them get through each day.
- Check online for the branch of the military your grandchild is in. Most branches have websites for military families that will give you a good idea of your grandchild's daily schedule and other information so you can pray effectively and purposefully for your grandchild. There may also be a weekly online newspaper or bulletin you can access that

will give you a more detailed briefing on what's happening where your grandchild is stationed. Your grandchild may be able to provide you with this information and any security clearance you might need.

• Don't try to send food or treats to your grandchild in the military. In most cases they will be confiscated.

Talking with Your Young Adult Grandchildren about Faith

Perhaps you have read articles or heard about today's emerging adults, many of whom have walked away from their childhood faith or have chosen a secular lifestyle and no longer attend church. Some of these reports are true. Researchers tell us that the number of emerging adults who consider themselves "nones" (when asked what their religious affiliation is, they respond with "none") is rapidly growing. This could be a description of your young adult grandchild.

There are many reasons why today's young people are less inclined to be involved in a church or other Christian ministries during their college years and beyond. Often they leave church because they have never been part of an adult church (they have only experienced children's ministries and youth groups), or they have become disillusioned with the church's political or cultural associations, or they have had trouble reconciling the Christian faith with secular ideas about science and technology. If you have a young adult grandchild, it might be helpful for you to read some good books that have been written on this subject, including *You Lost Me: Why Young Christians Are Leaving Church . . . and Rethinking Faith* by David Kinnaman, *Lost in Transition: The Dark Side of Emerging Adulthood* by Christian Smith et al, *Souls in Transition: The Religious and Spiritual Lives of Emerging Adults* by Christian Smith and Patricia Snell, or *Mere Science and Christian Faith: Bridging the*

Divide with Emerging Adults by Greg Cootsona. These books cover the subject very well and are based on good research as well as good thinking.

While it is true that many youth struggle with their faith as they enter their young adult lives of freedom and independence, it's also true that they have come to very few final conclusions about faith or lifestyle choices and probably won't for many years. They are on a journey—the process of coming up with a faith of their own, not their parents' faith or anyone else's. The good news is that for many emerging adults, the faith they eventually come to have can be more robust and sustainable than anything they believed as children. We must be able to trust the process and trust God.

Here are just a few tips for sharing your faith with your young adult grandchildren:

- Above all, don't condemn or criticize your grandchildren when they express doubts, disagree, or more passively avoid going out of their way to attend church or participate in church-related activities. This will make you even more of a long-distance grandparent than you already are. Your grandchildren will not want to talk to you if you criticize or condemn.

- Stay in touch with them. Don't cut them off because they aren't going to church or aren't behaving in ways you approve. Keep on sending those cookies and love notes.

- Let them know that you love them and are praying for them. However, avoid communicating things like "I keep praying for you . . . that somehow God will knock some sense into your head so you'll come back to Jesus." Instead, let them know that you are praying God's best for them in every way.

- Even if your grandchildren are not presently walking with the Lord, you can still share your faith with them. Just do it in loving, appropriate ways. Be who you are, speak the truth in love, and don't be afraid of rejection. Share what God is doing in your life. Let them know how you can see God working in their lives. Bless them and encourage them in every way.

- Ask questions and learn to listen. Let them know that they can talk to you about anything. Learn to be unshockable. When they ask a difficult question, don't try to answer unless you are certain of the answer you are giving. Don't argue, but share what you believe and know and then trust God for the outcome. If they raise questions about a particular issue, see what you can learn before your next conversation and share your thoughts.

- Remember that God is not finished with your grandchildren and that we may never live to see the day when they are walking with Christ. Of course, God isn't finished with us either, or our children, so we can trust God completely for our grandchildren. Of course our hope and prayer is that we will indeed see our grandchildren walking with Christ, and with us, in heaven.

For Further Reflection and Action

1. Were your grandparents still alive when you were a young adult? What kind of relationship did you have with them?
2. How did your faith and values change when you reached young adulthood?
3. When your grandchildren reach young adulthood, your role in their lives will likely change as well. But you will remain a very important influence in their lives. What are the best ways for you to stay connected and to support your young adult grandchild?

4. See if your local church has need of adult volunteers for their youth or young adult ministries (they probably do!) and get involved in some way. If you can get some experience understanding and mentoring emerging-adult youth in your church, you will be in a much better position to understand and mentor your own emerging-adult grandchildren.

8

The Cliffs Notes

Okay, we've covered a lot of ground in this book, and I've used a lot of words. So what's the bottom line? Well, let me give you the "Cliffs Notes," a quick ten-point summary or big picture of this book—and what long-distance grandparenting is all about.

1. **It's okay to be a long-distance grandparent.** Sure, it would be wonderful if all your grandkids lived right down the street, but that rarely happens in today's world. Our grandkids are more likely to be anywhere in the world than close by. Use that distance as a motivation to be very intentional about staying connected with your grandchildren. It will take some effort and some planning.

2. **Remember that your God-given role as a grandparent is to pass your faith in Christ on down the line**—to your children, and your grandchildren, and your great-grandchildren, if you live long enough to see them. You may have retired from your career, but you never retire from ministry to

your family. Always be thinking of ways you can teach your grandchildren about the love of God.

3. **There is no distance between you and your grandchildren when it comes to prayer.** Whether they are in the next room or in another country, you can pray for them just as effectively. When we pray regularly for our grandchildren, we transfer all of our concerns and fears and worries to God, who is always faithful and trustworthy. This allows us to enjoy our grandchildren, live in the moment, and know that God is in control of things. We can trust Him completely with our grandkids.

4. **Visit your grandchildren.** There's nothing better than being with your grandkids in person. This will take some advance planning and budgeting, especially if it involves flying or multiday trips. Make a big deal about your visit with the grandkids and start counting down the weeks and the days until you are able to make the trip. Spend dedicated time with the grandkids while you are there, and make it a happy, fun time for the whole family to be together.

5. **Invite your grandchildren to visit you.** Create a home away from home for your grandchildren where they will feel welcome and comfortable and will have plenty to do. Again, plan ahead and let your grandchildren know well in advance that you have some special activities scheduled and can't wait to see them. You might even consider inviting all the grandchildren for a summer camp experience at your home! Hopefully there will be many times when your grandchildren and their parents will come for a visit, but it's always special when the grandkids can be with you for some dedicated time alone.

6. **Plan special family gatherings or family vacations.** If you have the resources, a family reunion, a cruise, an anniver-

sary celebration, or an overnight trip to an amusement park can be a wonderful way to spend some quality (and fun) time with your grandchildren. Perhaps you can pool resources with family members to secure a good place to gather. There may be a special place—a town, a beach, a cabin, a campground—with some family history or other connections where memories can be created. Remember that sometimes these occasions for memory making can be wonderful relationship-building times for you and your grandkids.

7. **Use the phone, video calls, and other technology to stay connected.** We live in an incredible time—with more ways to connect with our loved ones than ever before. There's no way we can cover all the possibilities in this book because new ways are being created every day. Whether it's using the phone, sending an email, text messaging, or communicating via Skype, Marco Polo, or Zoom, find out what works best with your grandkids and do it.

8. **Send stuff.** Grandchildren love to get things in the mail. Letters, postcards, and packages with stickers, cookies, toys, games, books, money, and other gifts let your grandchildren know that you are thinking about them and that you love them. Your presence is always better than your presents, but tangible items you can see and hold in your hand often become a meaningful touchstone between you and your grandchildren.

9. **Be on the lookout for good resources** that you can use to share God's love with your grandkids. Whether it's coloring books, Bible lessons, storybooks, devotionals, videos, or other resources that are age appropriate, load up on some of the best that are available and keep them in your home or send them to your grandchildren to read or enjoy. You might even want to incentivize your grandchildren's

learning by offering to pay them for reading, completing lessons, or memorizing Scripture.

10. **Remember, something is always better than nothing.** Don't try to be the perfect long-distance grandparent. You will not only fail but your grandchildren may want to have you committed. Be yourself and do whatever you are able to do. Tell them about Jesus whenever it seems appropriate to do so. I can tell you from experience that grandparents don't have to live close to their grandkids in order to have a lasting impact. Do what is possible for you and then pray that God will bless your efforts. He loves our grandchildren even more than we do, and He is faithful.

For Further Reflection and Action

1. Has this book helped you as a long-distance grandparent? If so, I would love to hear your feedback. Email me at wayne@waynerice.com.

2. Which of the ten "Cliffs Notes" listed above is most helpful to you?

3. What is the "one thing" you will start doing as a result of having read this book?

4. Do you have good ideas of your own that you would be willing to share? If so, I can be contacted at wayne@wayne rice.com.

NOTES

Chapter 1: On Becoming a Long-Distance Grandparent

1. From a 2002 AARP study reported in Julia Halewicz, "Long-Distance Grandparenting," Scholastic.com, http://www.scholastic.com/browse/article.jsp?id=3750662.

2. "General Characteristics of Housing," United States Census 1940, https://www.census.gov/prod/www/decennial.html#y1940, accessed January 16, 2018.

3. Jim Rice, "Swingin' Bridge," copyright 1994. Used by permission.

4. Andrew D. Blechman, *Leisureville:Adventures in a World Without Children* (New York: Grove Atlantic, 2008), 5.

5. Marc E. Agronin, "It's Time to Rethink the Bucket-List Retirement," *The Wall Street Journal*, March 20, 2016.

Chapter 2: The Biblical Role of a Grandparent

1. Josh Mulvihill, *Biblical Grandparenting* (Bloomington, MN: Bethany House, 2018), 26.

2. Mulvihill, *Biblical Grandparenting*, 66.

3. Tim and Darcy Kimmel, *Extreme Grandparenting* (Carol Stream, IL: Tyndale House 2007), 13.

4. Quoted in Gary W. Moon, *Becoming Dallas Willard: The Formation of a Philosopher, Teacher, and Christ Follower* (Downers Grove, IL: InterVarsity Press, 2018), 187.

Chapter 3: The Prayer Connection

1. Paul Sailhamer, "Praying for Your Kids (and Grandkids!)" in *News-Break*, the newsletter of the First Evangelical Free Church of Fullerton, CA, January 18, 2004. Used by permission.

Chapter 4: The Personal Connection

1. Harriet Edleson, "Grandparents Who Move to Be Closer to Grandchildren," *New York Times*, June 28, 2015, https://www.nytimes.com/2015/06/27/your-money/grandparents-who-move-to-be-closer-to-grandchildren.html.

Chapter 5: The Long-Distance Connection

1. Jean M. Twenge, *iGen: Why Today's Super-Connected Kids Are Growing Up Less Rebellious, More Tolerant, Less Happy—and Completely Unprepared for Adulthood—and What That Means for the Rest of Us* (New York: Atria Books, 2017), 5.

Wayne Rice has been active in youth ministry, family ministry, and grandparenting ministry for more than fifty years. He is the cofounder of Youth Specialties, creator of Understanding Your Teenager seminars, former pastor to generations at College Avenue Baptist Church in San Diego, and currently the director of conferencing for the Legacy Coalition. Wayne has authored dozens of books, including *Junior High Ministry*, *Reinventing Youth Ministry [Again]*, *Generation to Generation*, and *Engaging Parents as Allies*. He received the Gold Medallion award from the Evangelical Christian Publishers Association (ECPA) for his book *Up Close and Personal: How to Build Community in Your Youth Group*. Wayne also plays the banjo. He and his wife, Marci, live in Alpine, California. They have three grown children and five grandchildren.

Josh Mulvihill is the executive director of church and family ministry at Renewanation, where he equips parents and grandparents to disciple their families and consults with church leaders to help them design Bible-based, Christ-centered children's, youth, and family ministries. Josh has served as a pastor for nearly twenty years, is a founding member of the Legacy Coalition, and has a PhD from the Southern Baptist Theological Seminary. He is the author of *Biblical Grandparenting*, *Preparing Children for Marriage*, and *Rooted Kids Curriculum and Worship*. Josh and his wife, Jen, live in Victoria, Minnesota, and have five children. For family discipleship resources, visit GospelShapedFamily.com.

More Foundational Grandparenting Resources

Many powerful voices are influencing our grandchildren, from those at home and in their schools to those in the world of entertainment and media. Dr. Josh Mulvihill gives you all the information, insight, and ideas you need to invest spiritually in your grandkids, from sharing with unbelieving grandchildren to discipling them to a mature faith. This book is perfect for individual use, with small groups, or in Sunday school classes. A DVD is also available for additional study.

Grandparenting and *Grandparenting DVD*

With depth and relevance, this leadership book places grandparenting ministry on a firm scriptural foundation. Ideal for pastors and church leaders, as well as for use in the classroom at seminaries, this resource is perfect for helping you show how grandparents can invest spiritually in their grandkids and speak wisdom and godliness into their lives.

Biblical Grandparenting

This brief and insightful book for church leaders offers practical guidance on how to begin a grandparenting ministry in your church. Discover tools and resources to help grandparents share their faith with and disciple a new generation.

Equipping Grandparents

BETHANYHOUSE

Stay up to date on your favorite books and authors with our free e-newsletters. Sign up today at bethanyhouse.com.

 facebook.com/BHPnonfiction   @bethany_house_nonfiction

@bethany_house